The Essential Hayek

by Donald J. Boudreaux

with a Foreword by Václav Klaus

Fraser Institute
www.fraserinstitute.org
2014

Date of issue: September 2014
Printed and bound in Canada

Cover design and artwork
Bill C. Ray

Library and Archives Canada Cataloguing in Publication Data

The Essential Hayek / Donald J. Boudreaux

Includes bibliographical references.
ISBN 978-0-88975-308-2.

Contents

To Bill Field, who introduced me to Hayek's work.

Foreword

by Václav Klaus

Those of us born in the twentieth century—the century of two destructive world wars and two equally ruinous periods of Nazism and Communism—particularly those of us born during the Second World War and who spent four decades under Communism, who tried at that time to understand what was going on, and who eventually had the courage to try to change it, had always been looking for a compass that would make possible some elementary orientation in life. On the one hand, we looked to social sciences for a theoretical description and explanation, to the works of important scholars, thinkers, and writers; on the other, we looked for consequential, consistent, inspiring, straightforward personalities, for role models whose lives were in line with their writings.

Friedrich August Hayek was absolutely crucial for many of us in both of these aspects.[1] Born in 1899 in Vienna, the capital of the Austro-Hungarian Empire, which was still under the rule of Emperor Franz Joseph I, Hayek took part in the First World War as a soldier on the Italian front. When he returned home to Vienna to complete his university studies, he found the empire lost, the borders in Europe redrawn, the country deeply shaken, and the economy in ruins (and experiencing a devastating hyperinflation). He started working in a government-run institution dealing with war debts under the auspices of another great Austrian economist, the one-generation-older Ludwig von Mises. Mises turned his attention to the Austrian School of Economics

---

1 See my "Hayek, the End of Communism, and Me," *CATO Policy Report* XXXV (5), 2013 <http://www.klaus.cz/clanky/3345>. This was originally the speech "Hayek and My Life," delivered at a conference at the University of Richmond in April 2013.

tradition and its powerful methodology (especially its theory of money and credit) and, with the formation of the Soviet Union and its central planning without markets and prices, to the suddenly highly relevant debate about the impossibility of economic calculation under socialism. Hayek developed and substantially enriched both topics in his writings in the following decades.

After moving to England and to the London School of Economics in 1931, in the era of the Great Depression, Hayek quite rapidly became the main opponent of John Maynard Keynes and his advocacy of massive state intervention as a necessary saviour of capitalism. Hayek sharply and uncompromisingly opposed the Keynesian doctrine, which he interpreted as the most dangerous vehicle because through it, the doors would be opened to full socialism. Many consider the dispute between Keynes and Hayek to be the main and most important controversy in the field of economics in the twentieth century.[2] For many decades—in fact until the period of stagflation in the 1970s—Keynes seemed to be the winner, at the least in practice, in the field of economic policy.

The Austrian School of Economics traditionally underestimates, if not neglects macroeconomics (or at least its importance), and Hayek understood that he was not going to win the debate accepting the Keynesian macroeconomic playground. He decided to attack the interventionist doctrine of Keynes by moving to microeconomics, to the defence of the irreplaceable role of markets and prices in the economy, and to demonstrating that interventionism makes the efficient functioning of markets impossible. His seminal articles "Economics and Knowledge," and especially "The Use of Knowledge in Society," are among the most important contributions to the field of economic science in the whole of the twentieth century. Hayek devoted his analysis to explaining the coordination of human action in a world in which knowledge is inevitably dispersed and he was able to prove that the solution is in the price system, not in central planning.

Hayek went further. His next move was to go beyond the boundaries of economic science. During the tragic Second World War, he saw not only Nazism in Germany (and his native Austria), and communism in Russia and the whole Soviet Union, but also the similar centralization of decision-making, government planning, and administrating of the economy, the

---

2 For example, Nicholas Wapshott (2011), *Keynes–Hayek*, W.W. Norton.

similar suppression of civil rights, and the similar introduction of all kinds of controls in all countries engaged in war. He considered this development a new tendency that had to be challenged. He did so in 1944 by publishing a non-academic book, *The Road to Serfdom* (dedicated to "the Socialists of all Parties"), which has become the most important text for all freedom-loving people since. I have to confess that it was almost a bible for those of us who lived for decades under Communism. Hayek turned our attention to the slippery road that descends from a limited, and at first sight almost "innocent" government interventionism, to an illiberal and unfree system. Liberty was for Hayek the essential value of Western civilization without which other values cannot be realized.

The Road to Serfdom became a bestseller (especially after its Reader's Digest version) and for Hayek opened the door to non-academic readers. He did not stop there. He continued his mission with an important organizational activity, founding the Mont-Pélèrin Society in 1947. The society gathered together a very influential group of classical liberals and other well-known opponents of interventionism and social-democratism. For almost seven decades since, the society has been meeting regularly and is responsible for the revival of liberalism in the second half of the twentieth century.

Frustrated at seeing the growing impact of Keynesianism in the 1950s and 1960s, Hayek more or less left theoretical economics and moved to more general (and less rigorous) fields—to political philosophy, law, the methodology of science, and even psychology. His topics were diverse, but their content remained very focused: freedom, its enemies, free markets, and the ambitions of constructivism. This change of topics can be easily discerned from the titles of his books and articles from that period: *The Abuse of Reason*; *The Sensory Order*; *Individualism: True and False*; *The Theory of Complex Phenomena*; *Evolution of Systems*; *The Atavism of Social Justice*; *The Counter Revolution of Science*; *Law, Legislation and Liberty*; etc.

Hayek spent most of the 1950s in the United States, a significant part of it at the University of Chicago (though to his frustration, due to the non-scientific character of *The Road to Serfdom* his time at Chicago wasn't in the prestigious Department of Economics). At the beginning of the 1960s, Hayek returned to Europe, to the University of Freiburg, and spent the last third of his active life in Europe where he really belonged.

In 1974, when he had stopped formally writing on economic topics, he got the Nobel Prize in Economic Science, which was an important justification and of great satisfaction to him. In his Nobel Prize speech, "The Pretence of Knowledge," he summarized his views about the difference between physical sciences and social sciences (including economics), and criticized attempts to use the methods of physical sciences in other fields. He called this attempt "scientism," not science.

In the last decades of his long life (he died in 1992, at the age of 93), Friedrich Hayek was involved in preparing, in a normative way, the outline of *The Constitution of Liberty*, (published in 1960), in which he tried to formulate the legislative preconditions for liberty (without trying to "sell" it to any political party). He became an advocate of evolutionism and "spontaneous order" (as opposed to constructivism). The contrast between "constructive rationalism" and "the evolutionary way of thinking" was absolutely crucial for him. He tried to show the impossibility of rationalist constructivism. To understand his emphasis on the difference between human action and human design is to understand Hayek.

Hayek was one of the most significant intellectuals of the twentieth century, but though he was extremely important for people in Western countries, he was not sufficiently appreciated and recognized there. I remember being in "his" Austria in November 1989, one day before the Velvet Revolution in my country, and hearing at the University of Linz that "Hayek is dead in Austria." I reacted by saying that we would bring him back to life in Prague again. I dare argue that Hayek was more important for us in the East than for people in the West. Westerners did see a real danger in Communism, but did not see that they were beginning the path down their own Hayekian "slippery road." They often considered his views overplayed and exaggerated. For us, Hayek was our guru, our teacher, our lighthouse, our compass in the depressing era of Communism. It was easier for Hayek to capture our hearts.

After the fall of Communism, in the optimistic era when the "end of history" doctrines (à la Fukuyama) dominated, Hayek was considered vindicated—yet ironically, his writings were increasingly forgotten, as though they were no longer relevant. He was heralded as a "proved-to-be-right prophet" (which was slightly illogical because he never believed that his views and proposals could win in the real world), but his ideas (and his warnings) seemed to belong to a different time. With the "advantage" of our Communist past, however, some of us knew that Hayek's writings are by no means less relevant than they were before.

Two decades after Hayek´s death history is on the move again. State interventionism is back and growing, the Reagan-Thatcher era long forgotten, as is the Communist era. State paternalism, regulation and control, social and environmental blocking of the functioning of markets, constructivism and dirigism are here again and, especially in Europe, are stronger than ever. We must get back to Hayek's teachings. We must once again take his books into our hands and try to spread his thoughts all over the world, because now they are as relevant as in the past.

This book is a good start. It starts us on the path of reintroducing Friedrich Hayek to new audiences who, even though they may not realize it, need his insights and teachings nearly as much as we did in the twentieth century. Much of the Western world is well down the "slippery road" Hayek warned about in his writings. Only by understanding the tragic trajectory that might unfold will they fully understand how urgent it is that we avoid the pitfalls of the past. This book a great resource for all who value liberty, but even more importantly, it is essential reading for all of those who are unaware of the many dangers that can befall a society that ignores the lessons of the past.

Václav Klaus

Václav Klaus is the Former President of the Czech Republic (2003–2013), currently President of the Václav Klaus Institute, Distinguished Senior Fellow of the CATO Institute, and Professor of Economics at the Prague School of Economics.

Introduction

Every economist has at least one hero. I have several. Adam Smith, the wise eighteenth-century Scottish moral philosopher who founded economics, is one of my heroes. Another is Frederic Bastiast, a nineteenth-century French scholar and statesman who used humour brilliantly to convey basic economic insights. Also among my heroes is my late colleague at George Mason University, James Buchanan. Buchanan won a Nobel Prize in 1986 for using economics to better understand politics.

Milton Friedman, the American economist who not only revolutionized economic scholarship in the twentieth century but who also spoke plainly and compellingly to the general public, is yet another of my heroes. So, too, is Julian Simon, the economist who taught us that the ultimate resource in any economy is not inanimate stuff such as land or petroleum or gold or iron ore but, instead, the human mind that is free to innovate.

But my greatest hero—by far—is Friedrich A. Hayek (1899–1992).

Born in Vienna on May 8, 1899, Hayek moved to England in 1931. While teaching and researching at the London School of Economics, Hayek became one of the world's most renowned economists even thought he was still only in his mid-30s. His fame grew from his research into the causes of what where then called "trade cycles," what we today call booms and recessions.

In the Greatly Depressed 1930s, of course, such research was especially important. And Hayek wasn't alone in researching the causes of booms and recessions. Another economist studying the same matter was John Maynard Keynes (pronounced "canes"). Yet Keynes's theory of booms and recessions was totally different from Hayek's. Not only were the two accounts of booms and recessions very different from each other at the purely theoretical level, they also differed in the implications they offered for government policies to deal with economic slumps. Keynes's theory promised that recessions, even deep ones like the Great Depression, can easily be cured by greater government spending. Hayek's theory, on the other hand, offered no hope that a slumping economy can be cured by any such easy fix.

Among professional economists, Hayek's theory went quickly from being celebrated to being scorned. Keynes's theory won the day.

Whatever the reasons for Keynes's victory over Hayek, that victory was total. Keynesian economics came to all but completely dominate the economics profession for the next 40 years and to win widespread acceptance among policy-makers. By the early 1940s Hayek was largely forgotten.

Hayek's time in the shadows, however, was brief. In 1944 he published a book that became a surprise best-seller on both sides of the Atlantic: *The Road to Serfdom*. In this now-classic volume, Hayek warned that attempts to centrally plan an economy, or even to protect citizens from the downsides of economic change, pave a "road to serfdom." Hayek showed that if government plans or regulates the economy in as much detail and as heavily as many of the intellectuals and politicians of the day were demanding, government must also regiment citizens and strip them of many cherished freedoms.

Hayek did not say (as he is often mistakenly accused of saying) that the slightest bit of government regulation inevitably leads to socialism and tyranny. Rather, his point was that the more intent government is on socializing an economy and regulating it in great detail, the greater are the number of individual freedoms that must be crushed in the process.

Although informed by Hayek's economic brilliance, *The Road to Serfdom* is not an economics book. It is instead a work of political philosophy, and it marks Hayek's turning away from writing exclusively about economics for professional economists, to writing about the nature of society for broader audiences. And the audience for *The Road to Serfdom* was vast. In the United States, the popular magazine *Reader's Digest* ran an abridged version of the book in 1945, which proved to be surprisingly successful. (*The Road to Serfdom* remains relevant and popular. Sixty-five years after its best-selling success with *Reader's Digest*, American television and radio host Glenn Beck praised *The Road to Serfdom* on his Fox News channel program. As a result, in June 2010 Hayek's 1944 book shot up to a number-one ranking on Amazon. com, where it stayed for a week.)

Along with his change from narrow economist to broad social scientist, Hayek moved in 1950 to the University of Chicago. During his 12 years at that institution, he was not a professor in the Department of Economics but, instead, in the Committee for Social Thought. While at Chicago Hayek wrote a second and more extensive book in defense of a free society: *The Constitution of Liberty*, which was published in 1960.

In subsequent decades, two more such "big think" books would flow from Hayek's pen: the three-volume *Law, Legislation, and Liberty* (published in the 1970s) and Hayek's final book, *The Fatal Conceit* (published in 1988). *Law, Legislation, and Liberty* shows Hayek at his most bold and pioneering. Volume I brilliantly explains the differences between unplanned orders (such as languages and market economies) and planned organizations (such as business firms and centrally planned economies). Volume II explains why the popular idea of "social justice" is meaningless. Volume III contains Hayek's most ambitious attempt to describe in detail what the legal and political structure of his ideal society would look like.

The greatest contribution of *Law, Legislation, and Liberty*, however, is Hayek's explanation of the fundamental difference between law and legislation. Influenced by the Italian legal scholar Bruno Leoni, Hayek argued that law is that set of rules that emerges "spontaneously," unplanned and undesigned. Law forms out of the countless interactions of ordinary people as they go about their daily lives. Legislation, in contrast, is a set of rules and commands that government consciously designs and imposes. Hayek believed that every good society must use a combination of law and legislation, but that much mischief is caused when the two are confused.

While still working on volumes II and III of *Law, Legislation, and Liberty*, Hayek was awarded the 1974 Nobel Prize in Economic Science. Sharing this award with the Swedish economist Gunnar Myrdal, Hayek finally was accorded the professional acclaim that he'd lost since his refusal, four decades earlier, to jump onto and ride the Keynesian bandwagon. Hayek's close friends tell how this award renewed his vigour to work. He would live for nearly 18 more years and for much of that time he remained as creative and as productive as ever. His last book, *The Fatal Conceit*, published in 1988, deepens his insights into the potential creative powers of a society governed by evolved rules rather than by the discretion of political officials or of democratic majorities.

* * *

In this short book I aim to convey as clearly as possible the gist of ten of Hayek's most important economic and political ideas. While I share Hayek's viewpoint on most such matters, I've done my best in the pages that follow to convey *Hayek's* ideas and perspectives rather than my own. Inevitably, and especially because no scholar has exercised such a long-standing and powerful influence on the way that I approach economics and how I "see" social reality, I surely, from time to time, confuse my own ideas and viewpoints for those of Hayek. I've tried to avoid any such confusion, but acknowledge up front that my efforts are unlikely to have been completely successful. Other Hayek scholars, therefore, can object to any number of interpretations that I've put here on Hayek's writings. My hope is merely that I've reduced such confusions to a minimum and that the confusions that do remain are understandable and, hence, forgivable.

I've also avoided throughout excessive mention of Hayek himself. The reader should read the following chapters with the understanding that *all* of the ideas in those chapters are Hayek's ideas (or, again, at least what I genuinely believe to be Hayek's ideas). And so especially in combination with my other goal of making this volume accessible to a wide audience, there is no academic-style footnoting and citation in the text.

Readers interested in exploring Hayek's works in greater depth are, of course, encouraged to read those works directly. I recommend starting with *The Road to Serfdom* or *The Constitution of Liberty*, although economic students might wish to start with Hayek's influential essay "The Use of Knowledge in Society," which has been reprinted in many places after originally appearing in the September 1945 issue of the *American Economic Review*. (This essay is also available free of charge on-line at http://www.econlib.org/library/Essays/hykKnw1.html).

Hayek wrote no autobiography. There are, though, several good intellectual biographies of him. Bruce Caldwell's 2005 *Hayek's Challenge* is especially good. Readers might also consult Eamonn Butler's 2012 *Friedrich Hayek: The Ideas and Influence of the Libertarian Economist*, and Alan Ebenstein's 2001 *Friedrich Hayek: A Biography*. But I emphasize: there is no better way to learn Hayek's ideas than to read Hayek directly.

Reading Hayek directly isn't always easy. His prose, while unfailingly proper and precise, features long sentences filled with several clauses. Yet it (at least as I read Hayek's prose) has an attractive cadence to it—if a cadence that becomes agreeable only after having read more than just a few pages! But if the reader will trust my judgment, I can attest that becoming more than passingly familiar with Hayek's works yields generous intellectual dividends.

Still, even Hayek's "popular" works, such as *The Road to Serfdom*, are quite academic. He was, through and through, a profound scholar and never a journalist or popularizer. I will have done my job in the following pages if you, the reader, come to understand some of the key ideas of this great thinker, and to understand the timeless relevance of these ideas for the evaluation and formation of social policy. If you are inspired to go on to read Hayek directly, all the better.

* * *

My gratitude in writing this slim volume is great. I thank Jason Clemens and his colleagues at the Fraser Institute for the invitation to write this book, and for their support throughout the project. I thank my colleagues and students over the years, both at Clemson University and George Mason University. These colleagues and students are too numerous to mention here without risking leaving someone out, yet they have all taught me much. I'm grateful for my long friendship and collaboration—not least through our blog Café Hayek (www.cafehayek.com)—with Russell Roberts, now of the Hoover Institution. I am grateful also for Bruce Caldwell's generous counsel early on in this project, as well as for the insightful and helpful criticisms and suggestions of three anonymous reviewers.

And I am thankful especially to my early mentor, Bill Field, who introduced me to Hayek's work. I still recall the day, nearly 40 years ago, that Bill handed me his copy of Hayek's *Individualism and Economic Order* and suggested that I read "The Use of Knowledge in Society." "You won't understand it all," he warned. "But read it anyway. You'll get enough of it to understand that you should re-read it in the future. It's jam-packed with layers of insights." Bill was right.

Donald J. Boudreaux

Donald J. Boudreaux is Professor of Economics at George Mason University, a Senior Fellow at the Fraser Institute, and Martha and Nelson Getchell Chair at the Mercatus Center at George Mason University.

Chapter 1

How we make sense of an incredibly complex world

Most of the advantages of social life, especially in its more advanced forms which we call "civilization," rest on the fact that the individual benefits from more knowledge than he is aware of.

Friedrich Hayek (1960). The Constitution of Liberty.
In Ronald Hamowy (ed.), *The Constitution of Liberty*, XVII
(Liberty Fund Library, 2011): 73.

Recent innovations have allowed people to read materials using a wide variety of mediums, including iPads, computers, and even phones. But the original and still most familiar format is paper and ink. Yet the complexity of the coordination required to allow people to read even in this simple format is hard to believe. It illustrates one of Hayek's most profound insights: the ability of society to organize itself based on the pursuit of individual interests.

You are now reading words that, for many of you, are transmitted through the medium of two of society's most familiar products: paper and ink. These products are so common that we take them for granted; their existence seems to be as natural a part of our daily reality as does the force of gravity. And ink and paper are so inexpensive that they are often available free of charge. (When your mail arrives today, it will likely contain several catalogs and flyers advertising this clothing store or that supermarket. The cost of printing these mailings is so low that merchants daily send them out by the jumbo-jet load, all free of charge to those of us who receive them.)

And yet the people whose efforts, skills, and specialized knowledge, and the detailed information that went into producing the very ink and paper now before you, number in the millions. The printed words you are reading were composed by me, the author of this volume. But without the help of millions of other people from around the world, nearly all of whom are total strangers to me and to you, this modest book—the very printed words now before your eyes—would be impossible.

Consider the ink. Where does it come from? Its colour comes from a dye made from chemicals that were extracted from roots, berries, or bark. Who found those roots, berries, or bark? That person had to know which specific roots, berries, or bark to find. Most roots, berries, and bark won't work. And just how are the colouring chemicals extracted from this vegetation? Today that extraction is done through a complex process involving a mix of industrial chemicals and complicated machinery. The dye is then mixed with water, resins, polymers, stabilizers, and preservatives.

To make even one vial of the simplest and least-expensive modern ink requires the knowledge and efforts of many, many people. There are those who find the appropriate vegetation, those who design the machines for extracting

the colourings, others who operate those machines, and another group of people who mix the extracted chemicals with the other ingredients in order to make the resulting liquid work well as ink. And these steps are only the beginning.

The machines used to extract the colourings from the roots, berries, or tree bark are powered by electricity. So we need knowledgeable electricians to equip factories with electrical wiring. Other specialists are required to design the electrical-generating equipment that sends electricity coursing through the factories' wires. In addition to each of these specialists, others must manufacture the wires themselves, a process that involves yet different specialists to find and mine copper, iron ore, and bauxite. And then even other specialists are necessary to perform each of the many steps involved in transforming these raw minerals into copper, steel, and aluminum wires.

And I've so far discussed only the ink. What of the paper? What kinds of trees are used to make it? Where are these trees found? Although neither you nor I know the answers to these questions, *someone* must know. Whoever those specialists are, they are essential to the existence of the printed page now before you.

In addition to those particular specialists, though, the production of paper requires countless other specialists—ones who know how to make the blades for the chainsaws used to cut down the trees; ones who know how to explore for the oil used to make the fuel that powers those chainsaws; ones who know what chemicals, and in just what proportions, must be mixed with the wood pulp in order to transform that pulp into paper; ones who know how to arrange for insurance on the factory in order to make the operation of that factory economically feasible; ones who know how to design, and others who know how to operate, the machines that package the paper for shipment to the printer's workplace. This list of different people each with specialized knowledge and information goes on and on and on.

No single person knows more than a tiny fraction of all that there is to know about how to make the ink and paper that you are now reading. What's more, no single person—indeed, not even a committee of geniuses—could *possibly* know more than a tiny fraction of all the details that must be known to produce the ink and paper that you now hold in your hands. The details that must be attended to in order to produce these products are truly so vast and complex as to be beyond human comprehension.

And yet, here they are—you're staring at them at this very moment: ink and paper.

These goods exist not because some great and ingenious human plan called them into being. Instead, they exist because of a social institution that encourages people to specialize in learning different skills, as well as to learn different slices of knowledge and gather different bits of information about the real world. This social institution also sends out signals to these hundreds of millions of specialist producers, informing each of them how best to use his or her special skills and knowledge so that the resulting outputs of the economy will satisfy genuine consumer demands—and do so at costs that are as low as possible.

If these signals are reasonably accurate, the loggers' activities are coordinated well with those of the paper mill: neither too few nor too many trees are cut down. And the paper-mill's activities are coordinated well with those of the printer: neither too little nor too much paper of the sort that you hold in your hands now is produced. Reasonably accurate signals also bring about coordination of the activities of book publishers and the reading public: the larger the audience for a particular book, the larger will be the numbers of that book that are printed. Books that have too small a likely audience to justify the use of paper and ink to produce will remain unproduced by commercial printers.

Through these signals, therefore, millions of producers all across the globe—business firms, entrepreneurs, investors, workers—are guided to act in ways that "mesh" productively with each other. We get affordable ink and paper—and also automobiles and laptop computers and antibiotics and sturdy housing and supermarkets full of food and department stores full of clothing. The list is very long indeed.

One of the most notable facts of life in modern market economies is that each and every one of the things that we enjoy as consumers is something that no person knows in full how to produce. This fact is true, of course, for marvels such as smart phones and transoceanic jet travel, but it's no less true for mundane items such as ink and paper. The production of each and every one of these things requires the knowledge of thousands or millions or even hundreds of millions of people. Yet there is no overarching plan to make all these activities come together productively.

Of course, each individual worker plans and consciously guides his or her actions. Each individual firm plans and manages its activities. There is conscious planning and adjustment going on at the level of each individual and each firm and each distinct organization. But there is no overarching—no "central"—plan for the whole. No conscious, central plan or blueprint knits each of the millions upon millions of individual choices, actions, plans, and slices of knowledge into the larger outcome of "the economy." That larger outcome is, as F.A. Hayek described it, spontaneously ordered.

But how? What exactly *is* this social institution that coordinates the choices and actions of so many people, each with different slices of knowledge and information, into an overall pattern of activities that works so remarkably well? The answer is voluntary exchange, or markets that are based on private property rights and freedom of contract. That is, for individuals to be able to exchange in markets (sell and buy) they must feel confident in the security both of their own property and that of those they exchange with, as well as in the legal system (contracts) within which they operate. And the prices that emerge on these markets through thousands, even millions of exchanges, are the crucial signals that guide us every day to make those economic choices that result in the complex and highly productive economy that we too often take for granted. Market prices, as we'll see in the next section, guide each of us to act as if we know about—and as if we *care* about—the preferences and well-being of millions of strangers.

Chapter 2

Knowledge and prices

We must look at the price system as such a mechanism for communicating information if we want to understand its real function ... The most significant fact about this system is the economy with which it operates, or how little the individual participants need to know in order to be able to take the right action.

Friedrich Hayek (1945). The Use of Knowledge in Society.

In Bruce Caldwell (ed.), *The Market and Other Orders*, XV

(Liberty Fund Library, 2014): 100.

Imagine a jigsaw puzzle of one billion pieces. These pieces are scattered randomly across a pasture that is one million miles square. If someone assigns to you the task of finding all these pieces, how would you do so?

One option is to search for each of these billion pieces by yourself. If you choose this option, you'll likely die before you complete the task. Even if you live for 95 years and begin searching nonstop for the pieces the moment you are born, you'd have to find one piece every three seconds to find them all before you die.

But suppose you enlist the help of 1,000 friends to fan out with you across the pasture, searching for the pieces. The task is now much easier. If each of you finds just one piece every 30 seconds, you and your friends together will complete the task in a little less than one year.

Of course, this task can be made even easier by enlisting the help of one million people or, better still, 100 million people. With 100 million people scouring the pasture for puzzle pieces, each person would have to find an

average of only ten pieces. And so, if each of these 100 million searchers finds a piece every 30 seconds, the task will be completed in a mere five minutes.

Human cooperation is powerfully productive. Still, in this example, simply collecting all the pieces of the jigsaw puzzle is not by itself a very valuable achievement. The puzzle must eventually be put together properly to justify the time and effort spent on finding all the scattered pieces.

Think of each jigsaw puzzle piece as a unit of information that is potentially useful for making the economy work successfully. One piece might be the information that deposits of bauxite exist in a certain location in Australia.

Another piece might be the information about which mining engineers are especially skilled at designing an operation for extracting bauxite from the ground.

A third piece is information about how best to transport the bauxite to a processing factory. A fourth piece is information on how to make a crucial part for the engine of the truck or the locomotive that will transport the bauxite. A fifth piece is how to design the roads or rails on which that truck or locomotive will be driven.

Clearly, the number of pieces of information that must be found and used for bauxite to become, say, the aluminum sheeting that forms the casing of the printing press that produced the pages that you are now reading is staggeringly large. It is a number far larger than the mere one billion pieces of the jigsaw puzzle in my example.

It's foolish to expect any one person (or small group of people) to find all the pieces of information necessary for the production of aluminum sheeting (and for the production of fuselages for airliners, the production of oven foil, the production of soda cans ... the list is long).

Not only is the mere *finding* of all the many pieces of information too difficult to entrust to a small group of people; so, too, is the task of putting these pieces together in a way that yields useful final products.

Let's now amend the example to make the jigsaw puzzle an even better metaphor for economic reality. Suppose that, unlike with regular jigsaw puzzles, each piece of this puzzle can be made to fit snugly and smoothly with any other piece. In this case, merely assembling all of the one billion puzzle pieces so that they fit together neatly is easy. But note that it is possible to create an unfathomably large number of scenes with these pieces.

Trouble is, only a tiny handful of these scenes will please the human eye. Most of the scenes will be visual gibberish. The challenge is to arrange the pieces together so that the final result is a recognizable scene—say, of a field of sunflowers or of a bustling city street. Only if the scene is recognizable is the assembled puzzle valuable.

Now imagine yourself standing alone before a gigantic table covered with these one billion puzzle pieces. What are the chances that you alone can put these pieces together so that the final result is a coherent visual image—a useful and valuable final result?

The answer is "virtually zero."

The number of different ways to combine these one billion pieces together is unfathomable—it rivals the number of atoms in the universe. So even if the number of possible valuable scenes is one million, that's still only a minuscule fraction of the gargantuan number of possible ways that this puzzle can be assembled. The vast majority of images that can be created by arranging and rearranging these one billion pieces will be meaningless and, hence, worthless.

The size and complexity of the puzzle ensures that putting a central planner (or committee of planners) in charge of assembling the puzzle won't work. There's simply no way that a planner, gazing at a huge pile of puzzle pieces, can foresee any of the possible meaningful pictures that might emerge once these billion pieces are assembled.

So the planner must *discover* what meaningful pictures are possible. Yet he can make this discovery only in the process of actually assembling the puzzle. This jigsaw puzzle doesn't come in a box whose cover depicts the final result.

Of course, the planner can't assemble all one billion pieces at once. At each point in time, the human limits of the planner's attention and capacity enable him to take notice of, and to fit together, only a tiny fraction of the billion pieces.

How can the planner know, as he proceeds, if the groups of pieces that he has so far assembled will or will not turn out to be part of a larger, meaningful picture? Are the five million pieces assembled so far, although the image they now depict looks like nonsense (say, a green glob), destined to become part of a meaningful image (say, a forest) once they are combined with another five million or another 500 million pieces? Or is the current assembly of the five million pieces destined to remain meaningless—impossible when fitted with the other pieces to be part of a meaningful, pleasing image?

How is the planner to sensibly choose whether to keep going with his current assembly or to start over? The best he can do is guess. Unable to see the future, the planner has no way to know if the image depicted by the five million pieces that he has assembled so far will prove to be useful or useless when they are combined with the remaining 995,000,000 pieces. Although all-powerful in deciding which pieces go where, the planner is flying blind.

Yet the planner faces a second insurmountable difficulty. Even if he somehow could foresee from the start what the final image will be if the puzzle is assembled correctly, the planner is incapable of arranging and re-arranging such a huge number of pieces in ways that will bring about this final, valuable image. The puzzle pieces are too many, and the ways that they can be combined with each other too great, to enable a planner to perform the assembly successfully.

Clearly, planning is a terrible way to assemble the puzzle. A far better way is to let the puzzle assemble itself.

Sounds odd. But what if each puzzle piece came equipped with a monitor that provides feedback on how likely it is that connecting at such-and-such an angle with this or that other piece would be a step on the way to creating a larger, meaningful, and beautiful picture? What if, for example, each piece *beeps* whenever it connects productively with another piece—that is, whenever it connects with another piece in a way that contributes toward making the eventual final outcome a beautiful picture? And what if the volume of each beep were determined by how likely it is that any particular connection of two pieces will help in producing a beautiful overall outcome? The more likely any particular connection is to work toward a successful overall outcome, the louder the beep.

Now, finally, imagine each of these billion puzzle pieces having a mind of its own, as well the ability to move by itself. Each piece loves hearing these beeps—and the louder the beep, the happier the piece.

This puzzle—strange as it seems—will assemble itself into a configuration that results in a meaningful and beautiful picture. It will self-assemble in this way without any of the individual pieces intending to contribute to this outcome.

Each individual piece is motivated only to connect with other pieces in ways that produce the loudest beeps. Opportunities to connect that result in no beeps will be avoided in favour of opportunities that produce at least soft beeps. And opportunities to connect that produce soft beeps will be rejected in favour of opportunities to connect that produce loud beeps.

As long as the loudness of the beeps corresponds to ways of connecting that result in a meaningful, beautiful picture, such a picture will be produced without any person (or any puzzle piece) intending to produce it.

This puzzle will "self-organize" into a beautiful whole that is far greater than the sum of the intentions of the individual pieces.

Of course, no real-world jigsaw puzzle has pieces that move on their own in search of beeping sounds. But carry this puzzle analogy over to the real-world economy. Each owner of private property has incentives to use his or her property in ways that produce the greatest return—the "loudest beeps," if you will. The landowner can connect with tractor manufacturers and farm workers to grow corn, or with architects and construction workers to erect a building on the land. The option he chooses is the one that screams most loudly to him "Choose me! I'll make the greatest contribution to your wealth!"

Likewise for the individual worker who owns only his own labour services. He will combine his labour with the labour and assets of those other private-property owners who promise him the largest return on his work effort—that is, who promise him the highest pay.

With each private-property owner seeking only the highest returns on the use of his or her property, an overall economic order is brought about as each owner directs his property toward those uses that pay the highest prices. Similarly, consumers seeking only to get as much satisfaction as they can from spending their income avoid inefficient suppliers (whose prices are relatively high) and patronize efficient suppliers (whose prices are relatively low). Inefficient suppliers either increase their efficiency or switch to other lines of production. Efficiency is improved and a complex pattern of productive uses of resources emerges (as Hayek said) *spontaneously*.

This order—this overall outcome—is intended by no one. It is spontaneous.

And because this unintended, spontaneous outcome emerges from the self-interested actions of owners of private property, each of these owners is made better off. No one is forced to do business with those whom he'd prefer to avoid, and—being free to take advantage of any and all existing opportunities—each person chooses those available opportunities that improve his lot in life by the greatest degree.

One of Hayek's deepest insights is that the signals received by private-property owners on how best to use their property come chiefly in the form of prices—the prices of some options *relative to* the prices of others. A worker offered $30 per hour for his labour time by factory X and $25 per hour by factory Y will likely choose to work for factory X because factory X pays relatively more than does factory Y.

Similarly, customers who offer to pay $50 per unit for the output of the factory are more likely to acquire that output than are customers who offer only $45.

Responding to prices in this way doesn't produce heaven on earth. But it does encourage millions of people to interact peacefully with each other in ways that are mutually beneficial.

No person, no council, no committee, no congress, no parliament plans this successful overall economic outcome. And that's a beautiful picture, one that shows that we can have economic prosperity without giving enormous power to government officials—officials who, being human, will always be tempted to abuse such power.

Chapter 3

Individual flourishing and spontaneous order

[T]he individuals should be allowed, within defined limits, to follow their own values and preferences rather than somebody else's; that within these spheres the individual's system of ends should be supreme and not subject to any dictation by others. It is this recognition of the individual as the ultimate judge of his ends, the belief that as far as possible his own views ought to govern his actions, that forms the essence of the individualist position.

Friedrich Hayek (1944). The Road to Serfdom.
In Bruce Caldwell (ed.), *The Road to Serfdom*, II
(Liberty Fund Library, 2007): 102.

If Betty the baker notices that the price of cupcakes is rising relative to the price of white bread, she will shift some of her effort—along with some of her flour, yeast, and space in her oven—from baking white bread to baking cupcakes.

From Betty's point of view, the higher price that she can now fetch for her cupcakes is a signal that she can earn more profits by baking and selling more cupcakes. From the economist's point of view, the higher price of cupcakes means that consumers now want additional cupcakes more intensely than they did yesterday. An extra cupcake produced and sold today creates more consumer satisfaction—or, to use economists' preferred term, more "utility"—than did an extra cupcake produced yesterday. The rising price of cupcakes reflects an important change in consumer wants. This rising price also motivates suppliers to respond in ways that meet those changing consumer wants.

Baker — we need
more cupcakes!

A market economy, then, achieves two important goals simultaneously. (By "market economy" I mean an economy in which there are no legal restraints on how far and in what direction prices can move; in which private property rights are secure; and in which people are largely free both to earn their incomes as they individually choose and to spend their incomes as they individually choose).

First, a market economy permits self-interested people to prosper economically only by serving the interests of others. The greediest businessman can profit only by offering consumers deals that consumers value. Likewise, the greediest consumer can get what he or she wants only by paying suppliers amounts that suppliers find attractive. Adam Smith, the Scottish philosopher who is the acknowledged founder of modern economics, famously described this process: "It is not from the benevolence of the butcher, the brewer, or the baker, that we expect our dinner, but from their regard to their own interest. We address ourselves, not to their humanity but to their self-love, and never talk to them of our own necessities but of their advantages."

Second, prices set in market economies "tell" people just *how* they can best serve others' interests. Prices are the single most important sources of information for producers and consumers on what they can expect from others in market economies.

As George Mason University economists Tyler Cowen and Alex Tabarrok describe it, "A price is a signal wrapped up in an incentive."

A market economy, therefore, expands the ability of each of us to pursue our own goals by harnessing the cooperation of others. Try as you might on your own, you could never get yourself from, say, Montreal to Vancouver in a mere five hours without the help of countless others. From the pilot who flew the jetliner, to the oil-field worker who helped produce the aviation fuel, to the engineer who assisted in designing the jet's engines, to millions of other specialized producers. Their efforts expand your range of choices; their unique knowledge and skills give you options to do that which you would never in a million years be able to do without them.

Clearly, this expansion by market economies of the range of options open to each of us is a central and marvelous feature of modern life. (Again, ask yourself how much of what you consume daily could you, personally, produce with only your own knowledge and your own hands.) But this option-expanding role of market economies serves more than narrow materialistic purposes. It also expands the range of our "higher" options.

With greater wealth, each of us can better afford—if we choose—to take more leisure. Likewise with education: markets (to the extent that governments allow them to operate) make education both more affordable and better over time. We denizens of modern market economies have access not only to more brands of beer and larger flat-screen TVs but also to sublime recordings of Bach cantatas and Verdi operas, to affordable volumes of Shakespeare and Tolstoy and Hemingway, to safe travel to historically significant cities such as Athens and Rome, and to medical and dental care that the likes of King Louis XIV, Queen Victoria, and even John D. Rockefeller never dreamed of.

Yet the market expands our range of individual choices in an even more profound way: by its very nature, a market economy is one in which individuals are not herded together and assigned tasks under a single plan. Unlike in a firm or other organization that pursues a single goal—such as "make as much profit as possible by producing and selling automobiles"—a market economy is not aimed at attaining one unitary goal to which everyone in society must subordinate her own desires and plans.

In a market economy only basic and abstract rules are enforced—chiefly, the laws of property, contract, and tort, along with criminal sanctions against the initiation of violence, theft, and fraud. And these rules are almost all negative, in that they do not tell individuals what to do but, rather, only what *not* to do. The result is that each individual has wide scope to formulate his or her own plans—and wide scope in choosing just how to pursue those plans—without having first to secure permission from some authority.

The laws and norms of what Hayek called "the Great Society" are not designed to maneuver individuals into particular places to achieve some over-all, grand, concrete social outcome. Nor are these laws and norms judged by how well they do any such maneuvering. The reason is that the Great Society is one that gives each person maximum possible scope to formulate and pursue his own *individual* plans; it is not a society in which people are treated as the means to some higher ends.

That the Great Society gives to each individual maximum possible scope to live as he or she sees fit is, perhaps ironically, one reason that many people dislike it. The Great Society itself offers no higher purpose to which people can commit themselves. The Great Society doesn't ask individuals to consciously come together in any thrilling collective endeavour.

Yet this fact doesn't mean that there are no higher purposes for individuals to pursue. In the Great Society each individual can choose and pursue his own purposes—including high and noble ones. And the individual can do so in league with as many other people as he can persuade to join him. Contrary to a popular assumption, therefore, higher purposes need not be supplied by "society." These purposes can be chosen and defined by individuals interacting peacefully with each other within the Great Society. And among the beautiful features of this fact is that no one is forced to work for goals that he finds disagreeable, offensive, unworthy, or unobtainable.

Perhaps ironically, by allowing the maximum possible freedom for each person to pursue his or her own chosen goals, the result is an overall social order that very much deserves to be described as "Great."

Chapter 4

The rule of law, freedom, and prosperity

The conception of freedom under the law ... rests on the contention that when we obey laws, in the sense of general abstract rules laid down irrespective of their application to us, we are not subject to another man's will and are therefore free.

Friedrich Hayek (1960). The Constitution of Liberty.

In Ronald Hamowy (ed.), *The Constitution of Liberty*, XVII

(Liberty Fund Library, 2011): 221.

As we saw earlier, our modern prosperity springs from the use of the knowledge of millions of diverse individuals spread across the globe. This knowledge is typically very detailed, local, and quickly changing. No government can ever collect such knowledge and then properly digest and productively act upon it. The only practical way we know to ensure that as much of this knowledge as possible is discovered, properly digested, and productively acted upon is to rely upon millions of people each to discover a few "bits" of this knowledge and then, individually, to put each of those bits to use. By dividing among millions of people the task of discovering and acting upon knowledge, no one person is overwhelmed with having to absorb and use more knowledge than is humanly possible.

It is important to understand that without freedom, individuals are confined to behave only in ways permitted by government authorities. Unfree people, therefore, have less scope and ability than do free people to search for and to act upon such detailed and local knowledge.

One important reason for dividing among millions of people the tasks of discovering and acting upon small bits of knowledge is that no central authority can know how to order these people about and know what they will discover. But how to ensure that free people—without being directed by some wise and all-knowing central authority—will actually find this knowledge and put it to productive use? How can we be sure that free people will not act selfishly in ways that further their own individual interests at the expense of the general welfare?

One part of the answer is that in fact we do expect people to behave in their own self-interest, but that that self-interested behaviour ends up working to everyone's benefit. In a market economy, producers want to become as wealthy as possible, but to do so they must compete against each other for consumers' patronage. This system rewards success at pleasing others (consumers) and punishes, with economic losses, the failure to do so. Another part of the answer, though, is the rule of law. The rule of law is a system of rules that are impartial and applied equally to everyone—even to government officials. If everyone is bound by the same rules, no one gets to bend those rules to his or her own advantage.

A rule is impartial if it is not formulated to achieve particular outcomes. An impartial rule only constrains people from acting in ways that are widely regarded as harmful. These are mostly "thou shalt not" rules rather than "you are hereby commanded" rules.

Rules of the highway are a good example. The rules of driving, such as speed limits and traffic lights, do not aim at directing drivers to particular locations. Specific destinations, as well as the particular routes that drivers use to travel to different destinations, are for each driver to decide. The rules of the road are not meant to determine where drivers go or how they get there. Instead, these rules are meant simply to give each driver maximum possible scope for getting to his destination, by whatever route he chooses, as safely and as reliably as possible while also ensuring the safety of all other drivers.

Supplying this assurance to each individual driver means holding every driver to the same rules. If some class of drivers (say, red-headed people) were free to ignore traffic lights, then the value of traffic lights to all other drivers would be greatly reduced. A driver approaching an intersection when the light in his lane is green would still have to slow down and look to ensure that no red-headed driver is barreling through the intersection. Traffic accidents would increase and traffic flow would slow down.

Holding all drivers impartially to the rules of the road results in every driver forming a reliable set of expectations about how other drivers will act. Every driver in North America expects all other drivers to drive on the right-hand side of the road. The result is that each driver can move faster because she is freed from the need to consciously be on guard against on-coming cars being driven in the left-hand lanes. The same is true for traffic lights, yield signs, stop signs, and the many other rules of the road that drivers routinely, and typically without thinking, obey. These rules of law-of-the-road direct every driver to act in conformity with every other driver's expectations.

Of course, the rules aren't perfect. Sometimes they are violated. And those violations every now and then result in traffic accidents. But the fact that drivers occasionally run red lights or drive on the wrong side of the road does not mean that the rule of law doesn't prevail on our streets and highways. If drivers are confident that the rules of the road will generally be obeyed, they won't hesitate to use their automobiles to travel to and fro in order to pursue their own individual goals.

But if drivers lose confidence that the rule of law will prevail on the road, then driving becomes a less useful mode of transportation. Red-headed drivers (as in my earlier example) who are entitled to run red lights might indeed arrive at their destinations sooner than they otherwise would, but the vast majority of people will find automobile driving to be less useful than it would be if the rule of law were universally applied. People will drive less and encounter more difficulties en route. The erosion of the rule of the law on the roads will obstruct the ability of people to achieve as many travel goals as they would if the rule of law were fully enforced and applicable to everyone.

What's true of the rule of law on the roads is true of the rule of law more generally. When all people, including the highest government officials, are bound by the same general and impartial rules, every individual enjoys the greatest possible chances of achieving as many as possible of his own chosen ends. True equality reigns.

This equality is equality before the law. It does not guarantee equality of outcomes. But it does mean that no person's or group's interests are given extra weight or are singled out to be discounted. The result is that no person's or group's interests are sacrificed so that other persons or groups might enjoy special privileges. In this way a society is truly one of law and not of men.

The actual move toward greater and greater equality before the law over the past 200 or so years, in turn, reduced the role of "identities," such as accidents of birth, of skin colour, or of religious affiliation in determining a person's success or failure in life. Success or failure came more to be determined by character and merit—that is, by success or failure at cooperating on equal terms with other people, especially in producing useful goods and services for the market. The rule of law, therefore, plays a key role in securing not only our freedoms but also prosperity for as many individuals as possible.

Chapter 5

Legislation is distinct from law

Legislation, the deliberate making of law, has justly been described as among all inventions of man the one fraught with the gravest consequences, more far-reaching in its effects even than fire and gun-powder. Unlike law itself, which has never been 'invented' in the same sense, the invention of legislation came relatively late in the history of mankind. It gave into the hands of men an instrument of great power which they needed to achieve some good, but which they have not yet learned so to control that it may not produce great evil.

Friedrich Hayek (1973). *Law, Legislation, and Liberty*, 1
(University of Chicago Press): 72.

The single most profound advance in our understanding of society was made in the eighteenth century by a remarkable group of Scottish philosophers, foremost of whom were David Hume and Adam Smith. These Scots explained that (to quote another Scot of that age, Adam Ferguson) "nations stumble upon establishments, which are indeed the result of human action but not the result of human design."

A good example is language. No one invented language. No person or council designed it. Each language *evolved* over the generations into the particular "shape"—vocabulary, grammar, syntax—that it has today. No genius or committee of the best and the brightest linguists invented, for example, the word "chair" to mean in English an object in which humans sit. No language designer decreed the word "merci" to convey the meaning that French speakers understand whenever they hear or say that word. Word meanings evolved over time through repeated use and experience. Likewise for each language's grammar and syntax.

Languages are unquestionably the result of human action—in this case our and our ancestors' countless individual efforts in particular circumstances to convey meaning to others. ("Watch out for that falling rock!" "I love you." "Take that hammer to your father.") But none of the thousands of natural languages that have existed in history is the result of human *design*. None of these languages—not English, not French, not Urdu, not Chinese, not one—was invented. And yet each language is a remarkably useful tool for people who speak it to communicate in complex ways with each other.

Of course, once a language becomes established it is common for lexicographers to *codify* that language in dictionaries, thesauruses, and books of grammar. Samuel Johnson's eighteenth-century *A Dictionary of the English Language* is an example of a famous codification of the English language. Such codifications, however, do not create any language. Samuel Johnson did not *create* English; he merely recorded it as he found it in its evolved state in the mid-1700s. If Dr. Johnson had written in his dictionary that the word "chair" means "to kill in cold blood," people would not suddenly have started using "chair" as a synonym for "murder." Instead, people would have simply regarded Dr. Johnson's dictionary to be untrustworthy.

What is true of language is also true of law. The great bulk of law that governs human interactions was not invented and designed by some great Law Giver. Instead, law emerged without centralized design. Law evolved.

The law against murder, for example, is not the product of human intention or design. There was never a tribe or society in which the intentional taking of the lives of peaceful members of that tribe or society was acceptable and became unacceptable only when and because some elders, a wise leader, or a popularly elected assembly pronounced such killing to be wrong. Such killing is, to use a phrase from Anglo-American law, *malum in se*—it is wrong *in itself*. People do not tolerate murder in their midst; in some form or fashion they take steps to prevent murder and to punish—usually very harshly—those who commit it. Such steps are taken even when there is no formal government to lead such efforts. The same is true for theft, fraud, arson, and many other violent and aggressive acts initiated against the persons and property at least of the people regarded to be citizens of the group.

Some of these laws might be rooted in humans' genetic make-up. (Parents naturally will go to enormous lengths to protect the lives of their children and to ensure that their children's killers are punished appropriately. Similar, if less intense, sentiments are naturally felt for other family members and friends.) Other laws might be based more on mere social and religious conventions—such as the law that women in western societies, unlike in some African tribal societies, never appear topless in public or that women in many societies must never appear in public with their hair uncovered.

What matters here is that every day we obey a vast set of rules that are not consciously designed.

Consider how parking spaces in shopping malls are allocated on busy shopping days. Suppose that you and several other drivers are cruising around a crowded parking lot, each in search of a parking space. You eventually spot a car just beginning to pull out of a space. You will likely stop a few feet behind that parking space and turn on your car's blinker in its direction. When another driver, also looking for a parking space, sees your stopped car with its blinker on, that other driver immediately knows that you are claiming that about-to-be-abandoned space. That other driver, although disappointed that she missed out on the space, will nevertheless drive past you to continue looking for a space; that other driver leaves the space for you to occupy.

In this everyday example, both you and the other driver are governed by law. The first person to stop his car near a parking space being abandoned and to put his blinker on in the direction of that space is widely recognized as having established for himself a temporary property right to that space. It is a right that other drivers generally recognize and respect.

This law is not written in any book. It was not designed by a committee of parking geniuses. It emerged, unplanned and unintended, in the course of human interactions. And it serves the useful purpose of peacefully allocating scarce parking spaces in ways that are widely accepted as being fair.

This example of spontaneously evolved law governing the allocation of scarce parking spaces is just one instance of evolved law. A much more significant body of evolved law is the *lex mercatoria*, or "Law Merchant."

When trade in the Mediterranean region began to rapidly expand a thousand years ago, disputes between merchants naturally occurred with greater frequency. There was, though, no single sovereign power with authority over all of these merchants who traded with each other—some of whom were in Genoa, others in Venice, others in Umbria, and yet others in the several other different independent political jurisdictions that were then spread throughout the Mediterranean region. Nevertheless, a highly complex and uniform system of law emerged in this large region to settle commercial disputes. This law is today known in the English-speaking world as the Law Merchant.

Two features of the Law Merchant are worth emphasizing here.

The first is that the Law Merchant evolved spontaneously out of the actions of merchants; it wasn't designed and imposed by a king, military general, or parliament. Routine merchant practices came to be known by the merchants and these routines created expectations in all merchants about how they and their fellows would act under different circumstances. But conflicts arose when these expectations were violated—either intentionally or unintentionally—or when new occurrences happened that were out of the ordinary. Merchants themselves established and manned courts to settle these conflicts. These courts generally ruled in favour of those parties whose actions were most consistent with established merchant practices—and, hence, these courts generally ruled against those parties whose actions were deemed to have run counter to established merchant practice.

In much the same way that lexicographers look to widely accepted and established meanings of words when declaring in their dictionaries the meanings of words, Law Merchant courts looked to widely accepted mercantile practices to settle disputes and declare the law in the cases before them. Through this process, law is created and modified by ongoing human practices and interactions, and this law is further refined and spelled out in decisions by these courts. The important feature for our purposes is that no one designed this law. It is the result of human action but not of human design.

A second feature of the Law Merchant is that it was widely obeyed *even though there was no government to enforce it*. For starters, each merchant typically had powerful incentives on his own to follow the law—in the same way that you have incentives to follow the law of allocating parking spaces in crowded parking lots. By "breaking the law," you risk retaliation by others. Other drivers honk angrily at you and perhaps even confront you face-to-face to scold you for your offense. (Violating the law of allocating parking spaces usually causes only minor problems for others, so the punishments typically inflicted on violators of this law—nasty looks, repeated horn blowing, a few angry words, and the like—are correspondingly minor.)

For merchants, violating the Law Merchant risked severe damage to their professional reputations. A trader who didn't pay his debts on time, or who refused a certain shipment of supplies in situations when established commercial practice required that he accept that shipment, was a trader who lost future opportunities to borrow and trade with other merchants. Because those future opportunities were valuable, merchants had strong personal incentives to maintain their reputations for being law-abiding. And the best way to get and keep such a reputation was actually to *be* law-abiding.

It's no surprise, then, that the historical record shows that even when merchants lost cases decided by Law Merchant courts they typically obeyed the rulings. The merchants obeyed not because the government forced them to obey; again, in most cases there was no government available to enforce a Law Merchant court's ruling. Merchants obeyed the courts' rulings because to disobey those rulings would damage their own reputations.

Today's method of allocating scarce parking spaces and the Law Merchant are just two of many examples of law that is created spontaneously and isn't necessarily written in statute books. Law is not always legislated, but it *is* generally obeyed.

Of course, in addition to obeying the many laws that are not consciously designed we obey also many rules that *are* consciously designed. Rules consciously designed by government are "legislation." We obey legislation, though, only because government will fine, imprison, or execute us if we do not obey. And while we might respect the authority of government, we respect and obey legislation only because it is created and enforced by government. Unlike law, the actions declared wrong by legislation are wrong only because government prohibits them. These wrongs are *malum prohibitum*—wrong only because government says they are wrong.

Importantly, however, the mere enactment of a piece of legislation doesn't necessarily give the legislature's intention the force of law. While legal rules need not be created by a sovereign authority and written in a statute book to operate as genuine law, it is also the case that rules written in a statute book ("legislation") are not necessarily binding.

For example, according to the written criminal code of the State of Massachusetts, it is a criminal offense for two unmarried adults to have consensual sex with each other. Yet despite the fact that this prohibition against consensual pre- and extra-marital sex was duly enacted by the Massachusetts legislature and is clearly written in that state's legislative code, consensual pre- and extra-marital sex among adults in Massachusetts is in fact not unlawful. No police officer in that state would arrest violators of this legislation. No judge or jury there would convict even those who confess to committing this "crime." And if by chance some completely out-of-touch police officer or court today *would* attempt to punish a couple for this "crime," the public outrage would be so great that that attempt would fail. Indeed, in such a case the public would regard the police officer and the court—not the couple—as having broken the law.

The importance of recognizing the distinction between law and legislation goes well beyond semantics. Its importance is twofold.

First, awareness of this distinction enables us to better see that socially beneficial rules of behaviour often emerge and are enforced independently of the state. It is a myth to believe that law is necessarily a product of conscious design by holders of sovereign authority.

Second, regardless of the merits or demerits of government's expansive use of legislation, the respect that we naturally feel for law should not unquestionably be extended to legislation. A corrupt or unwise government will legislate in many ways that are socially destructive. We should not confuse such government commands with law—or accord respect to legislation simply because it is commonly called "law."

Chapter 6

False economic security and the road to serfdom

But the policies which are now followed everywhere, which hand out the privilege of [economic] security, now to this group and now to that, are nevertheless rapidly creating conditions in which the striving for security tends to become stronger than the love of freedom. The reason for this is that with every grant of complete security to one group the insecurity of the rest necessarily increases.

Friedrich Hayek (1944). The Road to Serfdom.

In Bruce Caldwell (ed.), *The Road to Serfdom*, II
(Liberty Fund Library, 2007): 153.

Indispensable to the creation, maintenance, and growth of widespread prosperity is an economic system that uses scarce resources as efficiently as possible to create goods and services that satisfy as many consumer demands as possible. To the extent that the economic system encourages, or even permits, productive resources to be wasted, that system fails to achieve maximum possible prosperity. If, say, large deposits of petroleum beneath the earth's surface remain undetected because the economic system doesn't adequately reward the human effort required to find and extract such deposits, then people will go without the fuel, lubricants, plastics, medicines, and other useful products that could have been—but are not—produced from this petroleum.

The system that best ensures that resources are used as efficiently as possible is free-market capitalism—an economic system based on transferrable private property rights, freedom of contract, the rule of law, and consumer sovereignty. This last feature of free-market capitalism is the right of each consumer to spend her money as she sees fit. She can spend as little or as much of her income as she chooses (in order to save whatever she doesn't spend), and she can change her spending patterns whenever and in whatever ways she likes.

In short, consumer sovereignty means that the economy is geared toward satisfying consumers, not producers. This aspect of a market economy is important to emphasize because we are often told otherwise, namely, that a market economy is geared to benefit mainly producers. Yet in well-functioning economies producers—including entrepreneurs, investors, businesses, and workers—are not ends in themselves. Their activities, as valuable as these are, are means rather than ends. These activities are justified and valuable only if, only because, and only insofar as these produce outputs that consumers choose to buy. If consumers change their spending patterns (as they frequently do), producers must change to accommodate the new ways that consumers spend.

The freedom of producers to respond to, and even to anticipate, consumer demands is so vitally important for the success of the market economy that people often regard the case for economic freedom to be chiefly a case for the freedom of *business*. This is a mistake. At root, the case for economic freedom is a case for the freedom of *consumers*.

Of course, because maximum possible consumer freedom entails the freedom of entrepreneurs and businesses to compete vigorously for consumers' patronage, the defense of free markets often requires the defense of profits as well as of business's freedom to experiment with different ways of earning profits. Oil companies not allowed to earn sufficient profits from finding new oil deposits won't invest the resources required to find those deposits. Upstart entrepreneurs prevented by licensing restrictions from entering a profession will be unable to offer their services to consumers who might find those services appealing. The defense of profits and business freedom, though, is a defense primarily of the chief *means* that the market uses to ensure that consumers are served as well as possible.

The fact that each person's livelihood is tied disproportionately to what he or she produces rather than to what he or she consumes creates a practical problem, however. Each person, as a producer, works only at one or two occupations; each person earns an income only from one or two sources. Yet each person, as a consumer, buys thousands of different items.

A change in the price of any one or a few consumer goods has much less impact on the well-being of an individual than does a change in the price of what that individual is paid for what he produces or for the labour services he sells. As a consumer I'd obviously prefer that the price of my favourite hamburgers or music downloads not rise by 20 percent, but such price hikes won't harm me very much. In contrast, as a producer I'd suffer substantially if my income fell by 20 percent. I'm much more likely to complain bitterly about—and to resist—a fall in my income than I am to complain about and resist a rise in the prices of the things I buy as a consumer.

Politicians in democratic countries naturally respond to these concerns. People's intense focus on their interests as producers, and their relative inattention to their interests as consumers, leads them to press for government policies that promote and protect their interests as producers.

If government policies that protect people's interests as producers are limited to keeping them and their factories, tools, inventories, and other properties safe from violence, theft, fraud, and breach of contract, then there is no danger. Indeed, such protection of producers—along with assurances against their being taxed and regulated excessively—is essential for economic prosperity. Trouble arises, however, when government seeks to protect producers (including workers) from market forces—when government aims to shield producers from having to compete for consumer patronage. Such protection promotes not free-market capitalism, but crony capitalism.

For government to ensure that some producers—say, wheat farmers—suffer no declines in their economic well-being requires that it restrict the freedoms of consumers, of other producers, or of taxpayers. Special privileges granted to wheat farmers must come in the form of special burdens imposed on others.

Consumers who exercise their freedom to buy fewer loaves of wheat bread (say, because they have grown to prefer rye bread) will cause the incomes of wheat farmers to fall, and may even cause some wheat farmers to go bankrupt. To protect wheat farmers from this consequence of consumer sovereignty obliges government to take steps to artificially prop up the demand for wheat. To artificially prop up the demand for wheat requires, in turn, policies such as punitive taxes on rye farmers (to discourage them from producing so much rye), restrictions on the importation from foreign countries of rye, or even requirements that consumers continue to buy at least as much wheat bread today as they bought yesterday.

Whatever particular policies government uses to protect wheat farmers from the consequences of consumers' voluntary choices, this protection *must* come at the expense of others. Other people—either as consumers, as producers, or as taxpayers—are also made a bit less free by government's effort to protect wheat farmers from the downside of economic change.

If government protects only wheat farmers from competition—if government exempts only wheat farmers from having to follow the same rules of a market economy that are obeyed by everyone else—the resulting damage to the economy (especially in large advanced countries such as Canada and the United States) will be minimal. Wheat farmers will indeed each be noticeably better off as a result, while almost everyone else—as individual consumers or taxpayers—will suffer so little as a consequence that the pain might well go unnoticed.

Politicians will receive applause and votes and much other political support from wheat farmers without suffering a corresponding loss of popularity, votes, and political support from non-wheat-farmers. Politicians will then find it easy and attractive to gain even more political support by granting similar protection to some other producer groups—say, to steel workers or to airline pilots.

As government exempts more and more producers from the rules of the market—that is, as government relieves more and more producers from the necessity of having to compete, without special privileges, for consumers' patronage, and to enjoy the benefits of their successes and suffer the consequences of their failures—the total costs of such protection rise and, hence, become increasingly noticeable. The slowdown in economic growth for ordinary men and women becomes conspicuous. People grow more concerned about their economic futures.

Seeing government spread its protective net over an ever-increasing number of producers, those producers who haven't yet received such protection naturally begin to clamour for it. First, these producers understandably feel as though government is unfairly mistreating them by not granting to them what it grants to so many other producers.

Second, the greater the number of producers who are protected from the downside of economic competition, the greater the negative impact of that protection on consumers and the relatively few producers who are not yet protected. If the full burden of adjusting to economic change is focused on an increasingly smaller number of people, the extent to which each of those people must adjust is greater than if the burden of adjusting to economic change is spread more widely.

If government remains committed to protecting from the downside of economic change all who clamour for such protection, the powers of government must necessarily expand until little freedom of action is left to individuals. It is this stubborn commitment to protect larger and larger numbers of people from the negative consequences of economic change that Hayek argued paves the road to serfdom.

That government must have extraordinary discretionary power over vast areas of human action if it is to try to protect large numbers of people from the downside of economic change is clear. Any time entrepreneurs invent new products that threaten the market share of existing products the owners of the firms that produce those existing products will suffer lower demands for their services. So, too, will workers in the factories that manufacture those existing products. The incomes of these owners and workers will fall, and some might lose their jobs, as a result of the introduction of new, competitive products.

The very same process is true for *any* economic change. New imports from abroad threaten domestic producers of products that compete with these imports. Labour-saving technologies threaten the livelihoods of some workers whose human skills compete with the tasks that can now be performed at low-cost by these new techniques. Changes in population demographics—say, an aging population—cause the demands for some goods and services (for example, baby strollers and pediatric nurses) to fall as they cause the demands for other goods and services (for example, large sedans and cardiac surgeons) to rise.

Even simple everyday shifts in consumer tastes away from some products and toward other products unleash economic changes that inevitably threaten some people's incomes and economic rank. The growing popularity several years ago of the low-carbohydrate Atkins diet shifted consumer demand away from foods such as bread and beer and toward low-carb foods such as chicken and beef. As a consequence, bakers and brewers suffered income losses; ranchers and butchers enjoyed income gains. If government were intent on protecting bakers and brewers from experiencing these income losses, it would have either had to somehow stop people from changing their eating habits, or raise taxes on the general population to give the proceeds to bakers and brewers.

Regardless of the particular methods it employs, a government that is resolutely committed to protecting people from any downsides of economic change requires nearly unlimited powers to regulate and tax. As long as people have the desire and can find some wiggle room to change their lives for the better—for example, to change their diets, to invent technologies to conserve the amount of labor required to perform certain tasks, or to increase the amounts they save for retirement—some fellow citizens are likely suffer falling incomes as a result. The only way to prevent any such declines in income is near-total government control over the economy.

Unfortunately, because economic growth is economic change that requires the temporarily painful shifting of resources and workers from older industries that are no longer profitable to newer industries, the prevention of all declines in incomes cannot help but also prevent economic growth. The economy becomes ossified, static, and moribund. So achieving complete protection of all citizens at all times from the risk of falling incomes means not only being ruled by an immensely powerful government with virtually no checks on its discretion, but also the eradication of all prospects of economic growth. Inevitably, at the end of this road paved with the good intention of protecting all producers from loss lies not only serfdom but also widespread poverty.

Chapter 7

Economic booms and busts

In fact ... the very measures which the dominant "macro-economic" theory has recommended as a remedy for unemployment, namely, the increase of aggregate demand, have become a cause of a very extensive misallocation of resources which is likely to make later large-scale unemployment inevitable. The continuous injection of additional amounts of money at points of the economic system where it creates a temporary demand which must cease when the increase of the quantity of money stops or slows down, together with the expectation of a continuing rise of prices, draws labour and other resources into employments which can last only so long as the increase of the quantity of money continues at the same rate—or perhaps even only so long as it continues to accelerate at a given rate.

Friedrich Hayek (1974). The Pretense of Knowledge.

Lecture given in acceptance of the Nobel Prize for Economics.
In Bruce Caldwell (ed.), *Markets and Other Orders*, XV
(Liberty Fund Library, 2014): 367.

I. The role of "aggregate demand"

Business people know that their profits rise and fall with rises and falls in the demand for the products they sell. If more paying customers are streaming through the doors, times are good. Fewer customers, in contrast, mean worsening times—and, for many firms, even bankruptcy.

Likewise for workers. They understand that the greater the demand for their employers' outputs, the greater the demand for their labour services.

When business is booming, their jobs are more secure and their wages rise. When business is bad, jobs are less secure and wages stagnate.

This understanding by business people and workers of the importance of high demand in their industries and firms is correct. But as explained in the previous chapter, our roles as producers can mislead us into making mistaken conclusions about the larger economy. One such mistaken conclusion about the larger economy is that economic downturns—recessions—are caused by too little overall demand. A follow-up mistaken conclusion is that the appropriate cure for recessions is a set of government policies that increase demand.

Because an economy-wide recession affects nearly all firms and industries and not just a few, the demand that is said to be too low during recessions is called "aggregate demand." Aggregate demand is the *overall* demand in an economy for all goods and services.

The single most influential economics book written in the twentieth century is *The General Theory of Employment, Interest, and Money*, by the British economist John Maynard Keynes (1883–1946). Keynes reasoned that, just as high demand is key to the success of an individual firm, high *aggregate* demand is key to the success of a whole economy.

In Keynes's view, economic recessions are caused by too little aggregate demand. The cure for recessions, therefore, is higher aggregate demand. And the best way to increase aggregate demand is for government to ramp up its spending until economic health is restored—that is, until full employment is reached.

This Keynesian view is widespread. It seems to make so much sense. But it suffers serious flaws. And perhaps its biggest flaw is its focus on aggregate demand.

By focusing on aggregate demand, Keynesian economics ignores the all-important ("microeconomic") details of an economy. These vital details are how well or poorly each of the economy's many individual parts "fit" together and work together to generate goods and services for consumers, and to create job opportunities for workers.

If you have all of the parts of, say, an automobile scattered randomly about a large room, the main reason you do not have a functioning car is not that you do not want, or that you fail to "demand," such a car. Instead, the chief reason you have no functioning car is that those parts aren't fitted together in ways that allow them all to operate smoothly together so that a drivable and reliable car exists. It's true that no one will exert the energy and initiative required to assemble all of the parts into a working vehicle if there is no (or too little) demand for such a vehicle. But your *desire* to have a drivable car is not really the main obstacle standing between you and a working vehicle. The main obstacle is the challenge of mobilizing all the knowledge involved in assembling these pieces into a car *and* motivating people to put forth the effort to perform that assembly.

The desire of nearly everyone to possess and consume automobiles, along with lots of other goods and services, can be depended upon always to exist. The challenge is to ensure that producers have the knowledge and the incentives actually to produce the goods and services that people want. The challenge, in other words, is to get the economic *details* right so that producers have both the knowledge and the incentive to produce the "right" mix of outputs.

Relative prices are the main source of both this knowledge and these incentives. Relative prices are the prices of some goods and services *relative to* the prices of other goods and services. Examples are the price of a Toyota automobile relative to the prices of a Ford automobile and of a Honda automobile, or the price of a bushel of wheat relative to the prices of a bushel of rye and of a bushel of rice.

Relative prices are the most important "directors" of economic activity. If the pattern of relative prices accurately reflects the many different demands of consumers as well as the costs of the inputs that can be used to satisfy these demands, then entrepreneurs, investors, and consumers will be led by these prices to act in ways that result in all of the economy's "pieces" being fitted together into a productive whole. The economy at large will work pretty smoothly.

If, for example, consumers come to like oranges more than they had in the past, then the price of oranges will rise relative to the price of grapefruits. Farmers will soon produce more oranges and relatively fewer grapefruits. Or if supplies of iron ore fall, the price of steel will rise relative to the price of aluminum. Manufacturers will shift their production so that they use less steel and more aluminum to produce their products. If the price of gasoline rises, consumers will find ways to drive less, and they'll also buy more fuel-efficient cars. If the wages of nurses rise relative to the wages of school teachers, more young people will study nursing and fewer will study education. If interest

But how was I to know people didn't want
grapefruit anymore? I'm still charging 25 cents
a pound for them, like I did last year,
and the year before that.

rates fall, businesses will increase their investments in activities such as factory expansion, worker training, and research and development.

Changes in prices relative to each other directs businesses to increase their outputs of goods and services that consumers now demand more intensely (goods and services whose prices are rising) and to decrease their outputs of things that consumers no longer want as intensely as they did in the past (goods and services whose prices are falling). Importantly, the pattern of relative prices also "tells" businesses and entrepreneurs how to produce their outputs at the lowest possible costs. For instance, if the price of natural gas falls relative to the price of electricity, some business owners who would otherwise have used electricity to heat their factories or office buildings will instead use natural gas.

If the pattern of relative prices of consumer goods and services accurately reflects differences in the intensities of consumer demands for all of the different outputs produced in the economy—with prices rising for products in higher demand and falling for products in lower demand—producers will "know" what is the best mix of outputs to produce for sale to consumers. The pattern of prices tells them. And producers will have incentives to "listen" to these prices. The reason is that producers earn higher profits by expanding production of outputs whose prices are rising. Likewise, producers avoid losses by producing fewer of those outputs whose prices are falling.

Getting all of these details of pricing right is key to economic health.

In a competitive market economy based on private-property rights, people tend to make correct decisions. Not always, of course. But by and large the economic decisions people make in markets are sensible ones. The reason is that each individual personally gains by making wise choices about how to use his resources, and personally loses by making poor choices.

Our trust in the overall "correctness" of people's economic decisions, however, requires that the prices that people use to guide their decision-making are reasonably accurate sources of information. There's trouble if prices do not reflect realities. If consumers come to demand more oranges and fewer grapefruits, but the price of oranges doesn't rise relative to the price of grapefruit, citrus growers won't "know" to produce more oranges and fewer grapefruit. Too many workers and resources will be used to grow grapefruit; too few workers and resources will be used to grow oranges. These workers and resources will be *malinvested*—that is, these workers and resources will be invested in production processes that do not best meet the demands of consumers.

Likewise, if supplies of steel fall while supplies of aluminum rise, but the price of steel doesn't increase relative to the price of aluminum, produc-ers will not "know" to use less steel and more aluminum in their production plans. Shortages of steel will eventually arise, disrupting the production of goods that are made with metal.

If prices in only a handful of markets fail to accurately reflect underly-ing economic realities (such as the intensity of consumer demand for oranges relative to the demand for grapefruit), the economy won't suffer greatly. But when prices in general are out of whack—when prices in most markets send out *mis*information—widespread economic troubles arise. Entrepreneurs and investors throughout the economy will then act on false information about what consumers want and about what inputs make possible the lowest-cost ways to satisfy those wants.

With such widespread failure of prices to coordinate the plans of pro-ducers with the plans of consumers, economic activity stagnates. Some pro-ducers discover that they can't sell all of the output that they have produced. Other producers find themselves unable to get all of the inputs necessary to carry through with their production plans. Yet other producers learn that, had they produced more output, they could have sold more output.

If prices are free to adjust in response to these discoveries of errors, they will eventually do so. The pattern of prices will then give entrepreneurs and investors more accurate direction about what to produce and how best to produce those goods and services. Such adjustments in production activities, however, are not instantaneous. They take time. Orchards planted with grapefruit trees cannot immediately be transformed into orchards planted with orange trees. Redesigning an automobile body or the casing of MP3 players to be made with more aluminum and less steel can't be done with the snap of a plant-manager's fingers.

Unemployment rises during the time it takes for these adjustments to be made. Workers in industries with unsold inventories are laid off, and time is required for them to find employment elsewhere. Even industries that expand in response to more accurate prices typically require some time to rearrange their production plans and facilities in order to make profitable the hiring of new workers.

The time it takes for the firms to adjust away from the production plans they made when prices were inaccurate is time during which unusually large numbers of workers are unemployed.

Such unemployment is not caused by too little aggregate demand. Therefore, such unemployment cannot be cured by more government spending or other efforts to raise aggregate demand. Instead, such unemployment is caused by the widespread failure of individual prices to convey accurate information to entrepreneurs and investors about what specific products they should produce and about how best to produce these products. The only way to cure this malinvestment is to allow prices to adjust so that they better reflect consumer desires and the realities of resource availabilities. This cure, again, requires time—time for prices to adjust and for workers to find and move to jobs that are more economically sustainable.

II. The effects of poor monetary policy

What might cause such a widespread failure of prices to convey reasonably accurate information? The most likely culprit in reality is poor monetary policy.

If the money supply is stable—that is, if the money supply is not expanding or shrinking arbitrarily—the pattern of prices is likely to be mostly correct. There's no good reason to suppose that in an economy in which markets are reasonably competitive and well-working that, suddenly, prices *generally* will become so out of whack that significant amounts of labour and resources are drawn into industries where they don't belong. But if the money supply itself is changed, the pattern of prices might well become grossly distorted.

If the monetary authority (in most countries, a central bank with the power and authority to raise of lower the supply of money) injects streams of new money into the economy, significant distortions can occur. The reason is that new money enters the economy in particular places—specifically, through commercial banks making loans. This new money then spreads out to the rest of the economy from those places of entry. The people who are the first to get the newly created money spend it on particular goods and services. To make the explanation smoother, let's assume that the new money is spent first on purchases of new automobiles (by bank customers who use their borrowed money to finance such purchases).

The injection into the economy of streams of newly created money will thus cause the price of automobiles to rise relative to the prices of all other goods and services. These higher automobile prices tell an economic lie to people throughout the economy. Entrepreneurs and investors, seeing automobile prices rise relative to the prices of motorcycles, air travel, jeans, bread, and every other good and service, are misled into the false conclusion that there is a genuine increase in the demand for automobiles relative to the demands for other goods and services.

In fact, however, the higher prices of automobiles reflect only the fact that automobile buyers include lots of people who are lucky enough to be the first to spend the newly created money. This additional demand for automobiles isn't "real." This additional demand doesn't reflect people producing more output in order to earn more income to spend on new cars. Nor does this additional demand for automobiles come from these people decreasing their purchases in other markets in order to increase their purchases of automobiles.

In short, this higher demand for automobiles reflects only the fact that new money was created and spent, as it entered the economy, first on automobiles.

Once the stream of new money entering the economy stops flowing and these people no longer have this newly created money to spend, they will resume spending as they did before they got the new money. Demand for automobiles will fall back to its previous level (that is, demand for automobiles will fall to its level before being artificially driven up by the spending of the new money). But if enough new money is created and continually injected into the economy for a long-enough period of time, the prices of automobiles will rise by enough—and stay artificially high for long enough—to cause entrepreneurs and investors to shift some resources out of other industries and into automobile production.

Automobile producers will be the next in line to spend the newly created money. If automobile producers spend all of the additional money they get on, say, clothing, the prices of clothing will be the next to rise. Clothing sellers will, in turn, spend the new money that *they* get in some particular ways—say, on children's toys and kitchen appliances. The prices of children's toys and kitchen appliances will then rise.

Eventually, the newly created money works its way throughout the whole economy. This new money is ultimately spread out evenly across all markets. The final result is that the overall price *level*—that is, the average of all prices—is higher, but all individual prices *relative to each other* are unchanged from what they were before the new money was injected into the economy. For example, if as a result of the injection of new money the price of automobiles rises from $20,000 to $30,000 and the price of motorcycles rises from $10,000 to $15,000, the attractiveness to producers of producing automobiles relative to the attractiveness of producing motorcycles is unchanged: cars still fetch twice the price of motorcycles.

III. Where interest rates fit in

What's true for distortions in the relative prices of consumer goods (such as automobiles and motorcycles) is true also for distortions in the prices of consumer goods relative to the prices of capital goods (such as bulldozers and skyscrapers). Indeed, Hayek argued that distortions in the prices of capital goods in relation to consumer goods are the chief source of booms and busts. The reason has to do with the central role of one particular set of prices: interest rates.

Interest rates reflect people's "time preference"—that is, their preference for consuming today rather than delaying consumption until tomorrow. The lower is people's time preference, the more willing they are to delay consumption. And the more willing people are to delay consumption, the more they save. More savings, in turn, mean lower interest rates. (Banks have more money on hand to lend.) The lower are interest rates, the more attractive are long-term investments.

For example, a transcontinental railroad that takes ten years to build is a more attractive investment for the potential builder if the interest rate is 3 percent than if it's 10 percent. That's because the amount of interest that must be repaid when the railroad finally starts to operate and generate revenue will be much lower if the railroad builder borrows funds at an interest rate of 3 percent than at a rate of 10 percent. So although this railroad might not be profitable to build at the higher interest rate, it will perhaps be profitable to build at the lower interest rate.

Low interest rates signal to entrepreneurs that people in general are very willing to forego consuming today so that resources can be used to produce, not MP3 players, hot tubs, and other consumer goods today, but instead steel rails, locomotives, bulldozers, and other capital goods.

But what if people really *don't* want to delay their consumption for very long? What if interest rates "lie"—telling entrepreneurs that people are saving more than they really are saving? Hayek argued that such a lie plays an especially critical role in business cycles. When the money supply is increased, the new money typically enters the economy through banks—and to loan this new money, banks lower the rates of interest they charge borrowers. In Hayek's view, the prices that are most dangerously distorted by expansions of the money supply are interest rates. The artificially low interest rates prompt entrepreneurs and businesses to borrow too much—that is, to borrow more than people are really saving. Artificially low interest rates lead producers to undertake more time-consuming—"longer"—production projects than they would undertake at higher rates of interest.

Unfortunately, interest rates are lower not because people are saving more but only because the creation of new money pushed these rates lower. In this case, plans to build long-run projects—such as, again, a railroad that takes ten years to complete—will eventually run into trouble. With people saving too little to allow all of the necessary steel rails, workers' barracks, and other capital goods to be produced, the railroad builder in time finds that he cannot complete his project profitably. He must lay off his workers.

As time passes and the investments in excessively "long" business projects are finally entirely liquidated, laid-off workers find other jobs. This result, however, occurs only in the long run. Much economic trouble arises during the short run (which can be a long time when measured on a calendar). Once again, before all of the newly created money finally ("in the long-run") is spread evenly throughout the economy, the pattern of relative prices is distorted by the stream of new money injected into the economy. During the time it takes for the newly created money to work its way from the markets where it is first spent into each of the economy's many other markets, the distorted relative prices—including artificially low interest rates—mislead people into making economic decisions that are inconsistent with the true patterns of consumer demands and resource supplies.

It is regrettable that the process of unwinding unsustainable investments takes time. But lasting economic health requires that such unwinding occurs. Unfortunately, during the time required to unwind the unsustainable investments there is indeed a great deal of economic suffering. And, understandably, there are many appeals to political authorities to ease the suffering. As we'll see in the next chapter, political authorities too often respond to these appeals with policies that only mask and worsen the problem.

Chapter 8

The curse of inflation

Even a very moderate degree of inflation is dangerous because it ties the hands of those responsible for policy by creating a situation in which, every time a problem arises, a little more inflation seems the only easy way out.

Friedrich Hayek (1960). The Constitution of Liberty.

In Ronald Hamowy (ed.), *The Constitution of Liberty*, XVII
(Liberty Fund Library, 2011): 465.

Inflation is a decline in money's purchasing power. Inflation's most visible consequence is steadily rising prices of all or most goods and services in the economy. For a unit of money (say, a dollar) to lose purchasing power is for that unit of money to lose value. And when a unit of money loses value, it takes more units of that money to buy goods and services. In other words, the prices of goods and services bought with that money rise.

By far the most common cause of inflation is an increase in the supply of money. Just as the value of diamonds would fall if a freak meteorological event caused the skies to rain down genuine diamonds, the value of money falls when a nation's monetary authority increases the supply of that nation's money. Just as a rainstorm of diamonds would cause people who are willing to sell things in exchange for diamonds to demand more diamonds from buyers, an increase in the supply of money by the monetary authority causes people who are willing to sell things in exchange for dollars to demand more dollars from buyers.

The cause of inflation, therefore, is quite simple: excessive growth in the supply of money. Stopping inflation is likewise simple: quit injecting newly created money into the economy. But while stopping inflation is easy in principle (no complex theories must be mastered, and no intricate mathematical problems must be solved), it is often very difficult to stop in practice. The reason is that control of the money supply is in the hands of government officials. Stopping inflation is made difficult by politics, not least because it is politics that usually is to blame for starting inflation in the first place.

Since the demise of the gold standard in the twentieth century, governments have issued "fiat" money. Fiat money is money backed by nothing other than faith in the government that issues it. A government that issues fiat money will redeem units of that money only for other units of that money. The European Central Bank, for example, will redeem 20 euros only for 20 other euros. No gold, no silver, no anything other than itself backs fiat money.

One result of fiat money is to tempt government to finance some, and sometimes much, of its expenditures by creating money out of thin air. Because voters frequently and immediately resist having their taxes raised by enough to support every project that government officials want to fund—and because voters typically don't see the ill-effects of newly created money until much later—government officials often succumb to the temptation to pay for some of their preferred projects with newly created money.

As we saw in the previous chapter, however, money creation by government can cause serious problems down the road. The process of injecting newly created money into the economy can distort the pattern of relative prices and, hence, encourage an unusually large number of faulty economic decisions—that is, encourage an unusually large number of economic decisions that are revealed only later to be mistaken. Specifically, injecting new money into the economy causes too many resources to be invested in those industries that first receive the new money. Those industries over-expand.

Trouble arises when the truth is revealed that these industries over-expanded. When this revelation occurs, investors and entrepreneurs begin to eliminate what they now see is excess capacity in these over-expanded industries. Efforts to shrink these over-expanded industries, though, inevitably cause hardships. Most notably, unemployment rises as workers are laid off from their jobs in these industries.

During the time that unemployment is unusually high—during the time that it takes for these laid-off workers to find new jobs—political pressure is intense for government to "do something" about this unemployment. One of the easiest "somethings" that government can do is to keep the inflation going. By continuing to inject new money into the economy, government can for a bit longer prop up prices in the industries that are among the first to get the new money. In short, by continuing to inflate the money supply, government can postpone the discovery by entrepreneurs and investors that the industries that are among the first to get the new money are in fact over-expanded and burdened with excess production capacity.

The benefit to politicians of continuing to inflate the money supply is that, by delaying the discovery of the need to scale back over-expanded industries, they keep the economy *appearing* for a while longer to be healthier than it really is. These politicians, therefore, are at less risk of losing their jobs in the next election.

Economic reality, however, cannot forever be masked by the mere printing of more and more money. As the earlier streams of newly created money work their way through the economy to cause the prices of all goods and services to rise, inflation becomes expected. So for prices in the over-expanded industries to continue to be read by investors and entrepreneurs as signals that the increased investments in these industries are really not excessive, prices in these industries must rise even faster than before. Prices in these industries must rise at a pace greater than the expected rate of inflation.

To cause prices in these industries to rise faster than the economy's general rate of inflation, the central bank must quicken the pace at which it injects new money into the economy. If the central bank does so, prices in the industries that are first in line to get newly created money will remain higher than they "should" be relative to prices in other industries. Entrepreneurs and investors might then continue for the time being to believe that their increased investments in these "first-in-line" industries are justified. Efforts to scale back these industries are postponed. The unemployment rate, which would have risen today had there been no increase in the rate of monetary expansion, remains low. All looks well—for the present.

Eventually, however, the faster rate of money injection inevitably results in a faster rate of economy-wide inflation. Prices throughout the economy are now rising at a pace to catch up with the rising prices in those industries that are among the first to receive the newly created money. As a consequence, prices in these "first-in-line" industries stop sending out misinformation. These prices begin to reveal the fact that investments in these industries are indeed excessive—that productive capacity in these industries is too large. And so the only way the monetary authority can prevent investors from scaling back these industries and from laying off workers is to ramp up even more the rate of monetary expansion.

The monetary authority soon finds itself in a difficult spot. If it stops inflating the money supply (indeed, even if it simply fails to accelerate the rate of growth in the money supply), the industries that over-expanded because of earlier injections of new money will contract. The resulting rise in unemployment creates political pressures for government to "do something" to raise employment—something *other* than counseling the public to patiently wait while industries are restructured to be more economically sustainable. Accelerating the rate of inflation is one maneuver the government can take to keep employment high *for the present.*

But the increasing rate of monetary expansion leads to an increasing rate of inflation, which causes a host of other economic ills. These other ills include rising interest rates. (Bankers and other lenders will charge higher interest rates because they expect to be repaid next year in money of lower purchasing power than is the money they lend out today.) The other ills also include greater anxiety among workers that their wages will not keep pace with inflation—so workers demand higher wages today, ahead of the expected higher inflation. (The danger here is that if the rate of inflation turns out to be less than expected, workers' wages will have risen too high, causing some workers to lose their jobs or some employers to suffer unexpected losses.)

More generally, because monetary expansion does not cause all prices to rise in lock-step with each other, the higher the rate of inflation, the more distorted becomes the pattern of relative prices throughout the economy. The more out of whack individual prices become relative to each other, the less reliably do these prices guide entrepreneurs, investors, and consumers to make correct economic decisions. Higher rates of inflation, therefore, result in greater misuse (greater "misallocation") of resources. The economy's performance becomes worse and worse.

To cure this problem the monetary authority need only to stop injecting new money into the economy. But the cure isn't instantaneous. Not only does it take some time for people to stop expecting future inflation, but, also, it takes time for workers and resources to shift away from industries that over-expanded because of inflation and toward industries where these workers and resources will be more sustainably employed. By continuing inflation today, the monetary authority might be able to delay just a bit longer the need for over-expanded industries to shrink, but doing so also causes inflation throughout the economy to worsen.

Politically, the monetary authority might be thought of as having grabbed (as Hayek described it) a "tiger by the tail." While everyone agrees that a tiger ought never be grabbed by its tail in the first place, once someone *does* grab a tiger's tail, that person is at risk of being bitten and clawed when he lets go. But by holding on to the tiger's tail, he can delay facing the risk of being bitten and clawed. Holding on, though, only makes the tiger angrier, so that when it finally does break free—as it eventually will—the beast is even more likely to attack, and to attack with greater fury, the person who held its tail.

Help! I'll be killed if I let go—
and I'll be killed if I keep hanging on!

Understandably, at each moment in time, the person holding a tiger by the tail is tempted to hold on just a bit longer to delay the risk of being mauled by a big angry cat. Every moment of delay in letting go, however, only worsens the danger that will likely befall the person when he eventually does let go. And to make matters worse, at some point the tiger will become so furious that it will manage to break free on its own. The danger to the person who held on to the tiger's tail for that long will be enormous.

The difficulty of stopping inflation is very much like the difficulty of letting go of a tiger's tail. The mechanics of doing either task are incredibly easy: just stop printing money (to stop inflation) or relax the muscles in your hand (if you're holding a tiger by the tail). Yet in light of the anticipated consequences of stopping inflation or of releasing a tiger's tail, the task in either case is indeed challenging. In both cases performing the task requires not only the wisdom to see that continuing the current course will only make matters worse, but requires also the courage to confront the danger as soon as possible instead of delaying that confrontation.

Unfortunately—and here the analogy with holding a tiger by the tail breaks down—by continuing the growth of the money supply, many people in political power today can themselves *personally* escape any resulting political dangers. The bad effects of more inflation today won't materialize until sometime in the future, when many of today's officials will be out of office. So officials in office today can, by keeping the money supply growing, make the economy appear to be healthier than it really is, while the costs of creating this illusion will be borne only in the future by mostly different officials.

This political bias in favour of inflation is the chief reason justifying arrangements that strictly regulate changes in the supply of money. Returning to the gold standard is one option. Alternatively, the economist Milton Friedman (1912-2006) famously proposed a "monetary rule" that would prohibit central banks from expanding the money supply beyond some very small amount (say, by no more than three percent annually). Hayek himself came to favour denationalization of money—that is, getting government completely out of the business of issuing money and controlling the money supply. Competitive market forces would instead be responsible for supplying sound money. (Friedman himself, just before he died, became so skeptical of central banks that he argued that government be stripped of *any* power and responsibility to regulate the supply of money.)

Whatever the particular method used to eliminate political discretion over the money supply, eliminating such discretion should be among the highest priorities for those who seek an economy geared to solid, sustainable, and widespread economic growth.

Just as recovering alcoholics are wisely advised to avoid alcohol completely—and just as thrill seekers are wisely advised never to grab the tails of tigers—a people are wisely advised never to allow their government to exercise discretion over the supply of money. Following such a rule is the only sure way to avoid inflation and the many ills that it inflicts on an economy.

Chapter 9

The challenge of living successfully in modern society

Part of our present difficulty is that we must constantly adjust our lives, our thoughts and our emotions, in order to live simultaneously within the different kinds of orders according to different rules. If we were to apply the unmodified, uncurbed, rules of the micro-cosmos (i.e., of the small band or troop, or of, say, our families) to the macro-cosmos (our wider civilization), as our instincts and sentimental yearnings often make us wish to do, we would destroy it. Yet if we were always to apply the rules of the extended order to our more intimate groupings, we would crush them. So we must learn to live in two sorts of worlds at once.

Friedrich Hayek (1988). The Fatal Conceit.

In W.W. Bartley III (ed.), *The Fatal Conceit*, I

(Liberty Fund Library, 1988): 18.

As emphasized throughout this volume, modern prosperity is produced through an astonishingly complex web of human cooperation. This web of cooperation is vast. It spans the globe. Nearly every individual in the modern world is part of it, both as a consumer and as a producer. And so almost all of this productive cooperation is among strangers.

This fact is highly significant for the rules that guide us in our daily activities.

Every day, each of us participates in two very different kinds of productive and valuable social arrangements. One of these arrangements involves interactions with people who we know and care about—our parents, siblings, spouses, children, friends, close neighbours. Call these arrangements "small-group arrangements."

The other arrangements are with multitudes of strangers—the millions of people in the great global web of economic cooperation. A small handful of these strangers you see face-to-face, such as the cashier at the supermarket and the flight attendants on your most recent flight. But the bulk of these strangers—such as the person who sewed the shirt you're now wearing, and the person who designed the shoes now on your feet—are people you'll never lay eyes on. All of these strangers are people you know nothing about. Call arrangements with these multitudes of strangers "large-group arrangements."

One of the greatest challenges to those of us who live in modern society is to be able to function comfortably within *both* types of arrangements. The challenge lies in the fact that behaviours that are appropriate in one of these arrangements are often inappropriate in the other, and vice-versa.

Consider the ultimate small-group arrangement: the immediate family. As in the larger society, within families economic decisions must be made. What's on the menu for tonight's dinner? Who'll cook that dinner and who'll wash the dishes? (Such decisions allocate the family's labour resources.) Where will the family vacation this summer? Should money be spent to remodel the kitchen or should that money be saved for the kids' college education?

Within families, even such "economic" decisions are not made commercially among the members of the family. Perhaps family decisions are made by mutual agreement; perhaps mom and dad alone make all decisions. But regardless of the details of the rules or habits that any particular family uses to reach decisions, normal families do *not* make decisions by using "arms-length" formal contracting, market prices, competitive bidding, or any of the other impersonal procedures that characterize most of our economic relationships with strangers.

The same holds true for decision-making within other small-group settings, such as when friends decide which movie to watch together. The decision is typically reached by informal discussion leading to mutual consent, rather than through bargaining in which the highest monetary bidder gets to choose.

Also within families and many small groups we typically apply egalitarian norms of distribution. The portion of the family's budget that mom has, the portion that dad has, and the portion that each of the kids has is not determined by impersonal market forces. It is instead determined by a strong sharing norm. Within families, income is distributed not only consciously (usually by the heads of the household) but also more or less equally. This sharing norm within families and most other small groups is, of course, praiseworthy.

That we use informal, non-commercial decision-making procedures and norms in small-group settings is a good thing. First, the formalities and competitiveness of commercial procedures are unnecessary in small-group settings. Family members and friends genuinely care about each other and they know each other personally and with a depth of detail that simply cannot exist among strangers. So not only can people in small-group settings rely upon love or mutual concern to prevent cheating; people in these settings also know a great deal about each other. This mutual, detailed, and deep knowledge enables each person to be trusted to act wisely with respect to each other. Parents, for example, generally do not need to be forced by the police to treat their children well. Also, as parents they know their children's desires and abilities well enough that they do not need to learn this information through market competition and prices.

The close personal connections, the on-going face-to-face communications, and the mutual affections that bind together members of families and other small groups give each member of these small groups such deep knowledge of the other members that no impersonal means of dealing with each other are required.

Second and more importantly, using the formalities and competitiveness of commercial procedures in small-group settings would undermine all that is valuable about those settings. Central to our human nature is our longing and our ability to interact with loved ones and with friends on personal terms— to interact in ways that are built upon particular feelings and expressions of sentiment, caring, and love. Each of us wants to have people to personally care for and to care about, and each of us wants to be loved and cared for personally by other flesh-and-blood individuals. Attempts by parents, say, to charge their children for home-cooked meals, for the time that parents spend nursing their children through illnesses, or for any other benefits and care-giving that parents extend to children would rip from family interactions all that makes those interactions worthwhile and satisfying. Children growing up in such "families" would likely become, at best, social misfits as adults.

With the exception of giving young children an allowance as a way to help them begin to understand how to manage money, the money nexus has little or no place within a healthy family unit. A household run like a business would crush rather than nurture those familial bonds and personal sentiments that are so deeply important to us as human beings. In a world run *only* by arms-length contracting, market competition, money prices, and the formal "thou-shalt-not" rules that we follow when dealing with strangers, intimate relationships, loving families, and close friendships would not exist. Such a world would be worse than cold; it would be inhuman.

Everyone understands the value of personal relationships governed by love and sentiment. Not only are such relationships part of everyone's daily lives, we as a species are also evolved to treasure such relationships *and to know how to engage in them*. Again, parents naturally care for their children; they do not have to be instructed to do so or about how to do so. Likewise, because we humans spent most of our evolutionary history living in small bands of individuals who were known face-to-face to each other—and interacting only relatively rarely with strangers—nearly all of our successful *personal* connections continue to be with the individuals in our small groups.

The sentiments and emotions that bound members of small groups together and best enabled them to survive and to reproduce became encoded in our genes. These sentiments and emotions, therefore, are inextricably part of who we are. They are part of what it means to be human. And although human society in modern times has grown in size far larger than the small groups in which most of our ancestors lived, these small-group sentiments and emotions remain important "guides" to us in our dealings with our loved ones and friends.

As valuable and agreeable as these small-group sentiments and emotions are, however, they are poorly suited to guide us in our connections with the larger society. We cannot possibly know enough about strangers to be able to interact in their lives as intimately as we interact in the lives of people whom we know personally. Also, we cannot possibly care as deeply about the well-being of strangers as we care about the well-being of our family and friends.

And yet, to flourish in modern society requires our almost-constant interaction with countless strangers. To be productive for everyone involved, these interactions must be based on mutual consent and governed by an ethic of kept promises. But these interactions need not be based on feelings of love, caring, and concern. This fact is fortunate because, as just noted, no one is capable of knowing about and caring about more than a tiny number of the individuals with whom he or she interacts daily.

Being guided in our interactions with millions of strangers by impersonal rules and market forces, our capacity for love and concern for others isn't over-taxed. Nor are we called upon to learn the details of the lives of these strangers. When you want to buy, say, a new car, you need to know only some information about the quality of the car and its price in comparison with other cars. The only personal information you need to know when deciding whether or not to buy the car is information about *yourself*. What are *your* tastes and preferences in automobiles? What is *your* price range? What financial arrangements to pay for a car work best for *you*? You do not have to know—and you cannot possibly know—any such personal information about the millions of individuals whose efforts contributed to the production of the car.

The rules for interacting with strangers overlap with, but are much "thinner" than, the rules for interacting with people whom we know personally. Treat strangers with respect and do not presume that you are a better judge than they are of what is best for them; do not steal from strangers; do not cheat them; initiate no violence against them; keep your promises to them; respect their property rights. To follow these rules requires no personal knowledge of strangers. When people follow these impersonal rules when dealing with strangers in the economy, "arms-length" exchange and contracting occur. These exchanges and contracts give rise to market prices. These prices, in turn, guide each of us to interact productively—as both consumers and as producers—with the increasingly large numbers of strangers who make our modern lives possible.

The success and sustainability of modern society, therefore, requires that each of us be guided by our small-group norms when interacting with people we know personally, yet also to put those norms aside when interacting with strangers.

Switching back and forth between these two sets of very different norms is difficult, especially because we are genetically hard-wired to follow small-group norms. When we see on television or in Internet clips the faces of strangers who are suffering job losses or some other economic misfortune, our small-group norms trigger within us sympathies for these strangers (especially if they share our political nationality). So when government officials promise

to "do something" to relieve the suffering, we are inclined to support those efforts, even if we suspect that those efforts will cost us something.

Intellectual reasoning might convince us that the government's proposed efforts won't work, are too costly, or are otherwise unjustified. But insofar as we think of our nation as our extended family, the planned efforts of the government tap into our small-group norms. These norms, thus activated, are often difficult to overcome by those who wish to make unbiased ("rational") evaluations of government policies. For better or worse, even the best rational evaluation is often inadequate to overcome the emotional impulse to consciously tend to those among us who we perceive as suffering.

The power of these small-group norms is especially intense when government presents itself—and is portrayed by the media, by academics, and by popular culture—as being the caring and wise leader of our national "family." In the same way that we would make personal sacrifices to save our children or siblings from economic hardship, "we" as members of the national family, applaud efforts by the leaders of our national family to rescue those among us who have fallen on hard times.

But government policies springing from these small-group norms can be counterproductive. If, for example, government raises tariffs to protect the jobs of domestic wheat farmers, workers in other industries suffer. The reason is that higher tariffs on wheat—by reducing the number of dollars that foreigners earn by selling wheat to us—mean that foreigners will have fewer dollars to use to buy other goods from us (or to invest in our economy). But because these negative effects of the tariff are spread over a large and very diverse number of people, they are more difficult to see than are the benefits of the tariff, which are concentrated on a relatively small, uniform, and easily identified group of people. Being more difficult to see, these negative effects of the tariff don't trigger our small-group sentiments. Those sentiments, in short, bias us toward supporting policies whose beneficiaries are easily seen and whose victims remain cloaked in the complexities of reality.

Similarly, small-group norms of fairness that work well for determining the distribution of goods and resources within families and among friends are inappropriate for judging the distribution of goods and resources in the larger society. The forces that determine the relative sizes of people's bundles of material possessions in market economies are far more complex than are the forces that determine the sizes of people's bundles of resources within small groups.

In small groups, each person's effort, intent, and simple luck (good and bad) can be observed and taken accurately into account. You know, for example, if your brother's low income is the result of his bad luck or of his choices. (His low income, incidentally, might be the result of his *poor* choices—say, he drinks excessively—or the result of choices that are unobjectionable yet that yield only a low income—say, he chooses to earn his living as a street mime because he enjoys that line of work.) And you and others who know your brother can adjust how you treat him based upon your intimate knowledge of his particular circumstances.

In the larger society, in contrast, such personal observation and knowledge are impossible. No one can know every person's particular circumstances. Nor can we directly observe every person's contributions to the economy as a whole. The best available means of gauging the size of each person's contribution to the economy is to measure the monetary earnings he or she amasses in dealing peacefully in the market with customers, suppliers, and competitors.

The norms that we use in small groups are inappropriate for assessing the merits of the size of strangers' monetary earnings. What *appear* to us to be this stranger's unjustly high income and that stranger's unjustly low income in fact have layers of complex causes that cannot be observed and assessed with the sort of accuracy that we can attain when we observe and assess the justness of how much of a small-group's resources are claimed by each member of that group.

Another difference between small groups and large groups is important here. In small groups we can know with confidence most of the effects on our small group if we redistribute resources from one person to another—say, if mom and dad give Jane a bigger allowance and Joe a smaller allowance. In large groups, in contrast, we cannot trace out the full effects of redistribution. Because we can't comprehend all of the countless unseen interconnections and feedback loops that tie together the choices of millions of individuals from around the globe into the particular outcomes in which some individuals' annual incomes are relatively low while others' incomes are relatively high, we can't know the full effects of redistribution policies. Attempts to redistribute incomes in such complex settings risk triggering many negative feedback loops and upsetting productive arrangements that make even poorer those people with the lowest incomes.

Higher income taxes on the rich, for instance, might diminish private investment so much that over time the resulting loss in economic opportunities for the poorest citizens swamp whatever extra income they receive from government's redistribution policies. Likewise, redistribution might so stymie the incentives of today's poor people to stay in school or to find and keep jobs that the economic well-being of these people is actually worsened over time by the redistribution policies that are meant to help them.

The argument here is not that these particular negative effects will occur. Rather, the argument is that *some* unanticipated negative effects will occur if we try to make outcomes of the large group satisfy the sense of justice and fairness that are appropriate for our small groups. The reason is that our knowledge of the relevant details of the large group—our knowledge of the details of what Hayek called "the extended order"—is puny compared to our knowledge of the relevant details of our small groups. If we try to make the outcomes of the large group satisfy the notions of fairness and justice that are appropriate for small groups, we will dampen and distort the impersonal forces of competition and of profit and loss that are necessary in a large economy to allocate resources to uses that are of maximum value to multitudes of people. We will also weaken the obligation people feel to change their jobs and businesses if consumers no longer value the outputs of these jobs and businesses.

Switching back and forth between small-group norms and large-group norms isn't easy. It's understandable that many people feel a strong desire to apply small-group norms to the large group. Fortunately, however, for the past two or three centuries enough people in many parts of the world have avoided applying their small-group norms to the larger society and economy—or have avoided doing so at least enough to allow global, industrial, bourgeois capitalism to take root and spread. So it *can* be done. People *can* switch back and forth appropriately between small-group norms and large-group norms. Yet media and political commentary daily compound the difficulty of doing so.

In the next and final chapter of this book, we will explore the role of ideas and their inevitably dominant role in determining public policies. If our ideas are "good," they will overcome any sentiments we might have that are destructive to "the extended order." But if our ideas are "bad," the consequence will be policies that undermine and destroy the extended order and, along with it, our civilization.

Chapter 10

Ideas have consequences

The state of opinion which governs a decision on political issues is always the result of a slow evolution, extending over long periods and proceeding at many different levels. New ideas start among a few and gradually spread until they become the possession of a majority who know little of their origin.

Friedrich Hayek (1960). The Constitution of Liberty.

In Ronald Hamowy (ed.), *The Constitution of Liberty*, XVII (Liberty Fund Library, 2011): 177.

Karl Marx insisted that the ideas that you, I, and other people hold are shaped and powered by our station and function in the economy. Ideas themselves play no independent role in shaping the contours or in governing the destiny of an economy and society.

The great twentieth-century economist George Stigler (1911-1991) also believed that ideas have no consequences. In Stigler's view, every individual always seeks to maximize his or her own material well-being. Government officials, therefore, serve only those individuals and groups that best promote the well-being of government officials. According to Stigler, legislation and public policies are never the result of ideas or ideals. Instead, legislation and public policies are the result only of the interplay of narrow material interests— particularly the interests of groups that succeed in organizing themselves into effective political lobbies.

Marx, of course, was a man of the political left. Stigler was a man of the political right. Yet according to both Marx and Stigler, ideas are determined; ideas do not determine. Marx and Stigler each was driven by the idea that nothing as intangible, as subjective, as unobservable, and as unquantifiable as mere ideas could play a significant role in driving a society.

Marx and Stigler are not alone. Many are the scholars—especially in economics—who dismiss any suggestion that ideas independently affect public policy. In these scholars' view, the only forces that determine the performance of economies and the details of public policies are calculations of material personal profit and loss.

There are important kernels of truth buried within the idea that ideas are insignificant in the formation of public policies. Society cannot be formed into whatever ideas we might dream up, yet too many people throughout time have rejected this reality in favour of their utopian dreams. History has no shortage of schemes to rid societies of self-interest and material concerns, leaving the likes of love, universal brotherhood, or the assumed benevolence of powerful leaders to govern our affairs. All of these plans and schemes have failed. So to avoid being dazzled by the false promise of romantic and utopian schemes, we must never lose sight of the unavoidability of resource scarcities and of the reality of human nature—including the impossibility for each of us to know and care deeply about the millions of strangers who are part of our society.

This level-headed acceptance of reality, however, does not require that we reject the understanding that ideas have real consequences. Human beings are social animals, and ones with a remarkably sophisticated capacity for communication. We choose to live in groups and we are constantly talking and writing. And what are talking and writing if not a sharing of ideas? All this groupishness and incessant sharing of ideas means that we are influenced not only by what people do and by the details of our physical surroundings, but also by what people think—that is, by *ideas*.

No stronger evidence of the power of ideas exists than the fact that totalitarian governments, without exception, go to extreme lengths to control the ideas that people encounter. If ideas have no consequences, dictators and tyrants would spend no energy and treasure on preventing people from publishing whatever they please and saying whatever they wish. Nor would governments waste money on spreading propaganda. Freedom of expression would be universal if ideas had no power to determine what governments do and are prevented from doing.

Democratic governments with constitutionally limited powers also act as if ideas have consequences. Every piece of legislation, without exception, is trumpeted as promoting the public interest. Even statutes and regulations clearly aimed at helping only special-interest groups are packaged and presented to the public as vital measures for improving the condition of the overall society.

Consider, for example, farm subsidies that are driven by the disproportionate political power of agricultural lobbies. No politician ever says, "I voted for these subsidies because farmers are politically powerful and the consumers and taxpayers who foot the bill are not." If George Stigler were correct that government policies are driven *only* by special-interest groups—and therefore that the ideas that people have about the "rightness" or "wrongness" of policies are irrelevant—then governments wouldn't bother to portray farm subsidies and the creation of other special-interest-group privileges as being in the public interest. The very dishonesty and duplicity that is so common in the pronouncements of all governments, today and in the past, testify to the power of ideas.

There can be no doubt that ideas have consequences.

Ideas about the appropriate role of government determine what government will attempt to do as well as what it must refrain from doing. And ideas about the appropriate role of government are in turn shaped by ideas about the way free markets work and about the justice or injustice of market processes and outcomes. No society, for example, will follow a policy of free trade if a dominant idea in that society is that trade with foreigners is evil or economically harmful. In contrast, no society will tolerate high tariffs and other protectionist measures if a dominant idea in that society is that restrictions on trade are ethically unacceptable and that free international trade is always economically beneficial.

Getting ideas "right"—and spreading those right ideas as widely as possible—is therefore of the highest importance. Widely held mistaken ideas about markets and government will inevitably produce economically damaging policies, while correct ideas about markets and government will foster economically beneficial policies.

But how are ideas produced, spread, and nurtured? How are today's dominant ideas altered or replaced with other ideas? Families, churches, clubs, popular media, and (of course) schools all play a role. So, too, do public intellectuals—that is, newspaper and magazine columnists, bloggers, television and radio pundits, and book authors. Public intellectuals speak not only, or not even mainly, to other intellectuals; they speak chiefly to the general public. Being skilled specialists in communicating serious ideas to broad audiences, public intellectuals are the central participants in the process of distilling academic ideas into the language and forms that make those ideas accessible to the general public. Public intellectuals, as such, do not do original research or create new ideas. Instead, they report research findings and transmit academic ideas to people outside of the universities and think tanks.

Widely held ideas, then, about the operation of markets and about the promise or perils of government intervention have two main "producers": the scholars, researchers, and academics who generate these ideas, and the public intellectuals who transmit these ideas to wide audiences. If the general public in modern society is to hold improved ideas about markets and politics, both academics and public intellectuals must contribute to this betterment.

With the possible exception of history, no intellectual discipline plays as large a role in affecting the public's ideas about markets and politics than does economics. John Maynard Keynes astutely observed in 1936 that "[t]he ideas of economists and political philosophers, both when they are right and when they are wrong are more powerful than is commonly understood. Indeed, the world is ruled by little else. Practical men, who believe themselves to be quite exempt from any intellectual influences, are usually slaves of some defunct economist."

Original research and theorizing today, of course, affects almost nothing *today*. The ideas of professional economists must first be distilled and spread by public intellectuals, and this process takes time. A prime example is Adam Smith's scholarly case for free trade. When Smith first published his case for free trade in his monumental 1776 book, *An Inquiry into the Nature and Causes of the Wealth of Nations*, protectionist policies were well entrenched in Great Britain. These policies were so well entrenched that Smith thought it ludicrous to suppose that they would ever be discarded in favour of a policy of unilateral free trade. Yet on this matter Smith was wrong. Britain adopted a policy of free trade 70 years after Smith's ideas were first published.

Britain's adoption of free trade (which began in earnest with Parliament's repeal of the "corn laws"—tariffs on grains—in 1846) owes much to Smith's own scholarly case for free trade. The logic and eloquence of Smith's argument

Hmmm ... I never thought of it that way!
Perhaps I've been wrong.

inspired other scholars to do further research into trade. This research largely confirmed and strengthened Smith's conclusions. Just as importantly, it also inspired orators, pamphleteers, and other public intellectuals of the era to take up the cause of free trade. These public intellectuals explained to the public the benefits of free trade and the dangers of protectionism. By the mid-nineteenth century, public opinion in Britain had swung to free trade, along with other related free-market ideas. Not until the early twentieth century would Britain abandon free trade—an abandonment that itself was the product of intellectual developments some years earlier and that had been conveyed to wide audiences by public intellectuals.

Britain's experience with free trade and protectionism shows that if scholars get the ideas right, there's a very good chance that those right ideas will eventually influence public policies for the better. But the flipside is also true: if scholars get the ideas wrong, then public policy will eventually reflect those wrong ideas.

* * *

No economist in the twentieth century has done as much to get the ideas right as did F.A. Hayek. From his pioneering research into booms and busts, through his explorations into the role of prices and the essence of market competition, to his profound analyses of the rule of law and of the importance of principles both for guiding human actions and for constraining even the best-intentioned government policies, Hayek breathed much-needed new vigour into the case for a society of free and responsible individuals. Hayek's ideas not only continue to inspire original research by economists and other social scientists, but have become part of the discourse of many public intellectuals.

Hayek's ideas have already paid dividends. Margaret Thatcher, as Prime Minister of Great Britain, singled out Hayek for influencing her ideas about moving Britain away from collectivism. In the United States, Hayek's work was a key source of inspiration and guidance for the greater reliance in that country, during the last quarter of the twentieth century, on free markets.

As Hayek himself understood, however, the case for freedom and free markets must continually be rejuvenated and made again and again and again. The project is never completed, as more recent political developments in Britain and the United States attest. Opposing ideas—those of collectivism of one form or another—are always being generated, refined, and spread. Failure by classical liberals and other defenders of a society based on free markets and strictly limited government to counter these collectivist ideas will guarantee the victory of collectivism.

Being among the deepest and most profound ideas ever developed in the social sciences, Hayek's ideas can continually nourish the intellectual and moral case for freedom for many generations to come. It is my hope that this little book will play some modest role in introducing people to Hayek's ideas and in rousing them to build upon those ideas in order to help strengthen the sinews of a free civilization so that that civilization will not only endure, but grow to encompass the globe.

Suggestions for further reading

F.A. Hayek wrote so much—and so much has been written about him and his scholarship—that choosing a small handful of works to recommend to readers interested in learning more about Hayek is no easy task. The enormous size of this literature, though, means that there are many excellent works to choose from.

This short list of suggestions for further readings is divided into three parts. The first features works by Hayek himself. Choosing works for this section posed relatively little difficulty because most of Hayek's writings are aimed at specialized scholars (especially professional economists). Most are not works that non-specialists can easily dive into.

The second part contains suggestions for people whose only introduction to Hayek is this book.

The third part offers more "advanced" suggestions for readers who seek a greater depth of knowledge of Hayek's scholarship.

All works are listed along with their original dates of publication, although many of them have since been republished and often updated.

I. Hayek's own works

(1944). *The Road to Serfdom*. In Bruce Caldwell (ed.), *The Road to Serfdom: The Definitive Edition* (University of Chicago Press, 2007).

(1960). *The Constitution of Liberty*. In Ronald Hamowy (ed.), *The Constitution of Liberty: The Definitive Edition* (University of Chicago Press, 2011).

(2008). *Hayek on Hayek: An Autobiographical Dialogue*. University of Chicago Press. (Original work published 1944). <http://www.amazon.com/Hayek-Autobiographical-Dialogue-Collected-Works/dp/0865977402/ref=sr_1_1?s=books&ie=UTF8&qid=1402596565&sr=1-1&keywords=hayek+on+hayek>

(1976). The "New" Confusion about Planning. *The Morgan Guaranty Survey*. Reprinted in F.A. Hayek, *New Studies in Philosophy, Politics, Economics, and the History of Ideas* (University of Chicago Press, 1978: 232–246.)

(1976). Adam Smith: His Lesson in Today's Language. Reprinted as Chapter 8 in F.A. Hayek, *The Trend of Economic Thinking* (University of Chicago Press, 1991).

(1941). Planning, Science, and Freedom. Reprinted as Chapter 10 in F.A. Hayek, *Socialism and War* (University of Chicago Press, 1997).

II. For the beginner

Buckley, William F., Jr. (2000). The Courage of Friedrich Hayek. *Hoover Digest* 3 (July 30). <http://hooverinstd7dev.prod.acquia-sites.com/research/courage-friedrich-hayek>, as of June 18, 2014.

Buckley, William F., Jr., and Fritz Machlup, eds. (1976). *Essays on Hayek*. New York University Press.

Butler, Eamonn (2012). *Friedrich Hayek: The Ideas and Influence of the Libertarian Economist*. Harriman House.

Butler, Eamonn (1985). *Hayek: His Contribution to the Political and Economic Thought of Our Time*. University Publishers.

Caldwell, Bruce (2013). *Hayek's The Road to Serfdom: A Brief Introduction*. University of Chicago Press.

Ebenstein, Alan (2001). *Friedrich Hayek: A Biography*. Palgrave Macmillan.

Henderson, David R. (2008). Friedrich August Hayek. In *The Concise Encyclopedia of Economics*. On-line. Library of Economics and Liberty. <http://www.econlib.org/library/Enc/bios/Hayek.html>, as of June 18, 2014.

Miller, Eugene F. (2010). *Hayek's The Constitution of Liberty: An Account of Its Argument*. Institute of Economic Affairs.

III. For the more advanced reader

Barry, Norman P. (1998). *The Invisible Hand in Economics and Politics: A Study in Two Conflicting Explanations of Society: End-States and Processes*. Institute of Economic Affairs.

Feser, Edward, ed. (2013). *The Cambridge Companion to Hayek*. Cambridge University Press.

Peart, Sandra J. and David M. Levy (2013). *F. A. Hayek and the Modern Economy*. Palgrave Macmillan.

Schmidtz, David (2012). Friedrich Hayek. On-line. *Stanford Encyclopedia of Philosophy*. <http://plato.stanford.edu/entries/friedrich-hayek/>, as of June 18, 2014.

Publishing information

Distribution   These publications are available from <http://www.fraserinstitute.org> in Portable Document Format (PDF) and can be read with Adobe Acrobat® or Adobe Reader®, versions 7 or later. Adobe Reader® X, the most recent version, is available free of charge from Adobe Systems Inc. at <http://get.adobe.com/reader/>. Readers who have trouble viewing or printing our PDF files using applications from other manufacturers (e.g., Apple's Preview) should use Reader® or Acrobat®.

Ordering publications   For information about ordering the printed publications of the Fraser Institute, please contact the publications coordinator via:
- e-mail: sales@fraserinstitute.org
- telephone: 604.688.0221 ext. 580 or, toll free, 1.800.665.3558 ext. 580
- fax: 604.688.8539.

Media   For media enquiries, please contact our Communications Department:
- 604.714.4582
- e-mail: communications@fraserinstitute.org.
- website: http://www.fraserinstitute.org

ISBN   978-0-88975-308-2 — Printed and bound in Canada.

Date of issue   September 2014

Citation   Boudreaux, Donald J. (2014). *The Essential Hayek*. Fraser Institute.

Cover design and artwork   Bill C. Ray

Illustrations   Leslie Lightheart

Supporting the Fraser Institute

To learn how to support the Fraser Institute, please contact:

- Development Department, Fraser Institute,
  Fourth Floor, 1770 Burrard Street,
  Vancouver, British Columbia, V6J 3G7 Canada
- telephone, toll-free: 1.800.665.3558 ext. 586
- e-mail: development@fraserinstitute.org.

Purpose, funding, and independence

The Fraser Institute provides a useful public service. We report objective information about the economic and social effects of current public policies, and we offer evidence-based research and education about policy options that can improve the quality of life.

The Institute is a non-profit organization. Our activities are funded by charitable donations, unrestricted grants, ticket sales, and sponsorships from events, the licensing of products for public distribution, and the sale of publications.

All research is subject to rigorous review by external experts, and is conducted and published separately from the Institute's Board of Trustees and its donors.

The opinions expressed by the authors are those of the individuals themselves, and do not necessarily reflect those of the Institute, its Board of Trustees, its donors and supporters, or its staff. This publication in no way implies that the Fraser Institute, its trustees, or staff are in favour of, or oppose the passage of, any bill; or that they support or oppose any particular political party or candidate.

As a healthy part of public discussion among fellow citizens who desire to improve the lives of people through better public policy, the Institute welcomes evidence-focused scrutiny of the research we publish, including verification of data sources, replication of analytical methods, and intelligent debate about the practical effects of policy recommendations.

About the Fraser Institute

Our vision is a free and prosperous world where individuals benefit from greater choice, competitive markets, and personal responsibility. Our mission is to measure, study, and communicate the impact of competitive markets and government interventions on the welfare of individuals.

Founded in 1974, we are an independent Canadian research and educational organization with locations throughout North America and international partners in over 85 countries. Our work is financed by tax-deductible contributions from thousands of individuals, organizations, and foundations. In order to protect its independence, the Institute does not accept grants from government or contracts for research.

Nous envisageons un monde libre et prospère, où chaque personne bénéficie d'un plus grand choix, de marchés concurrentiels et de responsabilités individuelles. Notre mission consiste à mesurer, à étudier et à communiquer l'effet des marchés concurrentiels et des interventions gouvernementales sur le bien-être des individus.

Peer review—validating the accuracy of our research

The Fraser Institute maintains a rigorous peer review process for its research. New research, major research projects, and substantively modified research conducted by the Fraser Institute are reviewed by a minimum of one internal expert and two external experts. Reviewers are expected to have a recognized expertise in the topic area being addressed. Whenever possible, external review is a blind process.

Commentaries and conference papers are reviewed by internal experts. Updates to previously reviewed research or new editions of previously reviewed research are not reviewed unless the update includes substantive or material changes in the methodology.

The review process is overseen by the directors of the Institute's research departments who are responsible for ensuring all research published by the Institute passes through the appropriate peer review. If a dispute about the recommendations of the reviewers should arise during the Institute's peer review process, the Institute has an Editorial Advisory Board, a panel of scholars from Canada, the United States, and Europe to whom it can turn for help in resolving the dispute.

Editorial Advisory Board